Review

ON
MANAGING
HIGH-TECH INDUSTRIES

THE HARVARD BUSINESS REVIEW PAPERBACK SERIES

The series is designed to bring today's managers and professionals the fundamental information they need to stay competitive in a fast-moving world. From the preeminent thinkers whose work has defined an entire field to the rising stars who will redefine the way we think about business, here are the leading minds and landmark ideas that have established the *Harvard Business Review* as required reading for ambitious businesspeople in organizations around the globe.

Other books in the series:

Harvard Business Review on Brand Management

Harvard Business Review on Breakthrough Thinking

Harvard Business Review on the Business Value of IT

Harvard Business Review on Change

Harvard Business Review on Corporate Strategy

Harvard Business Review on Effective Communication

Harvard Business Review on Entrepreneurship

Harvard Business Review on Knowledge Management

Harvard Business Review on Leadership

Harvard Business Review on Managing People

Harvard Business Review on Managing Uncertainty

Harvard Business Review on Measuring Corporate Performance

Harvard Business Review on Nonprofits

Harvard Business Review on Strategies for Growth

Harvard
Business
Review

ON

MANAGING

HIGH-TECH INDUSTRIES

A HARVARD BUSINESS REVIEW PAPERBACK

The *Harvard Business Review* articles in this collection are available as individual reprints. Discounts apply to quantity purchases. For information and ordering, please contact Customer
Service, Harvard Business School Publishing, Boston, MA 02163.
Telephone: (617) 783-7500 or (800) 988-0886, 8 A.M. to 6 P.M.
Eastern Time, Monday through Friday. Fax: (617) 783-7555, 24
hours a day. E-mail: custserv@hbsp.harvard.edu.

Library of Congress Cataloging-in-Publication Data
Harvard business review on managing high-tech industries.
     p.   cm. — (A Harvard business review paperback)
    Contains articles previously published in the Harvard
business review.
    Includes index.
    ISBN 1-57851-182-8 (alk. paper)
    1. High technology industries—Management.   I. Harvard
business review.   II. Series: Harvard business review paperback
series.
HD62.37.H37 1999
620′.0068—dc21   99-18896
                                               CIP

*The paper used in this publication meets the requirements of the
American National Standard for Permanence of Paper for Printed
Library Materials Z39.49-1984.*

Contents

Technology Integration:
Turning Great Research into Great Products   1
MARCO IANSITI AND JONATHAN WEST

When Is Virtual Virtuous?
Organizing for Innovation   31
HENRY W. CHESBROUGH AND DAVID J. TEECE

The New Logic of High-Tech R&D   55
GARY P. PISANO AND STEVEN C. WHEELWRIGHT

Real-World R&D:
Jumping the Product Generation Gap   91
MARCO IANSITI

How Architecture Wins Technology Wars   117
CHARLES R. MORRIS AND CHARLES H. FERGUSON

Increasing Returns and the New World of Business   147
W. BRIAN ARTHUR

Building Effective R&D Capabilities Abroad   171
WALTER KUEMMERLE

Defining Next-Generation Products:
An Inside Look   199
BEHNAM TABRIZI AND RICK WALLEIGH

About the Contributors   223

Index   229

Harvard
Business
Review

ON

MANAGING

HIGH-TECH INDUSTRIES

Technology Integration

Turning Great Research into Great Products

MARCO IANSITI AND JONATHAN WEST

Executive Summary

IN MANY INDUSTRIES, superior technology Integration—the approach used to choose and refine the technologies employed in a new product, process, or service—is the key to achieving superior R&D productivity and speed, and superior products. Access to great research is still immensely important, but if a company selects technologies that don't work well together, it can end up with a product that is hard to manufacture, is late getting to the market, and does not fulfill its envisioned purpose.

In this article, which is based on an ongoing study of R&D in various segments of the global computer industry, Marco Iansiti and Jonathan West contend that technology integration has become much more important—and challenging—for obvious reasons. The number of technologies from which companies can choose has burgeoned. Both the breadth of technologies in a product or process and the potential sources of those technologies have increased considerably. Product life cycles have shortened dramatically, forcing companies to develop and commercialize new technologies faster than ever. As a result, the advantage now often goes to the companies most adept at choosing among the vast array of technologies and not necessarily to the companies that create them.

A radical change in the approach of U.S. companies to technology integration helps explain the resurgence of the U.S. electronics industry in the 1990s. But one size does not fit all. Indeed, the authors have found that an approach that works well in one country may not be the best for another. To be effective, an approach must suit the local culture and conditions.

IT'S LITTLE KNOWN, but one of the breakthroughs that led to the seemingly miraculous comeback of the U.S. electronics industry in the 1990s was the obscure process of technology integration. Business analysts often focus on the amount a company spends on R&D as an indicator of its competitive strength. But a company's process for rapidly and efficiently translating its R&D efforts into products that excel in satisfying the market's needs is much more important. After all, what a company gets for the money it spends on R&D is what ultimately matters. In many industries, superior technology integration is the key to achieving superior R&D productivity and speed—and superior products.

Technology integration is the approach that companies use to choose and refine the technologies employed in a new product, process, or service. Access to great research is still immensely important, but if a company selects technologies that don't work well together, it can end up with a product that is hard to manufacture, is late getting to market, and does not fulfill its

No company today can research every relevant discipline the way IBM and AT&T did during the 1970s and early 1980s.

envisioned purpose. An effective technology-integration process starts in the earliest phases of an R&D project and provides a road map for all design, engineering, and manufacturing activities. It defines the interaction between the world of research and the worlds of manufacturing and product application.

Technology integration has always been important, but in the past ten years it has become much more important—and challenging—for obvious reasons. The number of technologies from which companies can choose has grown dramatically. Advances in chemistry, information technology, electronics, and materials science, for instance, mean that the technological bases of many industries are changing rapidly and unpredictably. In many industries, the breadth of technologies in a given product has increased dramatically, too. A computer workstation, for example, employs knowledge from almost every field of the physical sciences and mathematics—from the physics of nuclear decay, which is needed for the design of dynamic random-access memory (DRAM) chips, to the mathematics of graph theory, which is relevant to its software. No single com-

pany today can research every relevant discipline the
way IBM and AT&T did during the heyday of the mainframe in the 1970s and early 1980s.

At the same time, the sources of new technology
have also proliferated. Graduates from leading universities populate the R&D organizations of companies all
over the world. Their
expertise in science and
technology has been fuel-
ing the growth of a wide
range of suppliers around
the globe that are familiar
with the latest innova-
tions. Any company can
tap those sources, so all companies must constantly
monitor the places that could spawn the next breakthroughs. If a market leader misses an important
source or fails to spot a market gap, challengers will
quickly seize the opportunity.

The advantage now often goes to the companies most adept at choosing technologies, not to the companies that create them.

To make life even tougher, product life cycles have
shortened dramatically, forcing companies to develop
and commercialize new technologies faster than ever. In
the semiconductor industry, for example, product life
cycles shrank by 25% in the 1980s alone. At the same
time, uncertainty in the marketplace has soared. Consider the computer industry, in which market requirements change extremely rapidly and customers have a
seemingly insatiable thirst for performance. By the mid-
1990s, few could predict with any confidence how the
Internet, the price of DRAM chips, or the emergence of
Java as an Internet scripting language would shape customers' demands even six months into the future. As if
all that complexity and uncertainty were not enough,
computer companies also have to contend with a mind-

boggling array of standards and manufacturing processes.

The competitive game has changed: the advantage now often goes to the companies that are most adept at choosing among the vast number of technological options and not necessarily to the companies that create them. What's it like to compete in such a world? Consider the following examples.

Intel's newest chip-manufacturing facility cost close to $3.5 billion, most of which was for production equipment—a third of which had never been used before. That third included novel approaches to lithography, etching, and planarization, which would allow Intel to squeeze the width of circuits below the wavelength of light. The manufacturing process comprised more than 600 steps, all of which had to work together perfectly to achieve high production yields.

Microsoft faced an equally daunting task in creating its Windows 95 operating system. One targeted feature of the product was that users be able to "plug and play"— that is, attach any peripheral to their computers and have the system work perfectly. To achieve that goal, each of the technologies employed in Windows 95 would have to function seamlessly with an almost unimaginable number of hardware and software combinations. The operating system would have to include literally millions of instructions and a wide range of technological approaches. Microsoft and Intel both had to figure out how to start with a large number of technological possibilities, each of which could have an uncertain impact on a very complicated system, and quickly come up with a product that would work reliably and coherently.

Unilever faced a similar challenge in the early 1990s, when it set out to improve the performance of its laundry detergents in order to gain an advantage in its mature but highly competitive market. Its challenge: to find a combination of compounds that would substantially and visibly improve the quality of wash in, say, both Italy and England, where consumers' behavior and the characteristics of washing machines differ considerably. Unilever bet that manganese compounds would improve the performance of detergents. But how could the company make sure that the new compounds would work safely and effectively in all situations?

Creating novel technologies was not the biggest problem facing Intel, Microsoft, and Unilever. The companies' internal research organizations and external suppliers could provide many new possibilities. Nor was the development of products and production processes the major challenge. These well-oiled organizations boasted managerial processes that would ensure speedy implementation once the technological path was laid. The main challenge was choosing among the vast array of technologies.

In an ongoing study of R&D in various segments of the global computer industry, we have made some discoveries about technology integration that offer lessons for other industries buffeted by massive technological novelty and complexity.[1] One discovery is that the process of technology integration is critical to competitive performance. Indeed, changes in the process were a key reason for the resurgence of U.S. manufacturers of computers, electronic components, and software in the 1990s.

Each segment of the computer industry that we have been studying—mainframes, high-performance workstations, semiconductors, and software—has faced different challenges, such as the enormous capital investments needed for semiconductor production and the extreme uncertainty of the markets for workstations and multimedia. In each case, a company's ability to choose technologies wisely has had a large impact on the performance of its R&D organization in terms of time to market, productivity, and product quality. In large mainframe projects, for example, differences in technology integration processes explained variations of as much as a factor of three in R&D productivity; at some companies, weak technology-integration processes caused delays of several years in developing new products. In workstations, companies with excellent technology-integration processes brought new products to market as much as two times faster than did competitors with less effective processes.

A company's approach to technology integration must fit its capabilities and local culture.

Our data suggest that differences in the technology integration process are more important than disparities in project management methods, leadership qualities, and organizational structure in explaining variations in performance. There are two reasons for this phenomenon. The first is that many of the most effective ways of organizing and managing projects have already been adopted throughout the world in this fast-moving industry. The second is that if an organization chooses the wrong technologies, the project will run into problems regardless of any other factor.

Another important discovery about technology integration is that there is not just one successful approach. Rather, to be successful, the approach adopted must be in harmony with a company's capabilities and its local culture and conditions. Our research in the semiconductor industry documents these ideas in detail. But before we delve into the evidence, let us explore how technology integration works.

A New Approach to R&D

In 1990, even the mightiest U.S. players in the computer industry were in retreat, and a lot of the weaker players had disappeared. IBM had lost substantial market share to Japanese manufacturers in every hardware segment. Intel was consistently late in introducing new generations of semiconductor technology and new chip designs. And even Microsoft's competitive position in software seemed in jeopardy as a result of severe delays in introducing new products as well as problems with product reliability.

A scant five years later, however, the U.S. industry had regained lost ground in such critical segments as semiconductors, personal computers, workstations, servers, and laptops. Intel and Microsoft had consolidated their leadership in microprocessors and software, respectively. IBM had improved its development and manufacturing capabilities and had introduced a wide variety of impressive new products. And a fresh generation of start-ups such as Netscape and Yahoo! had staked out the latest growth segments: Internet software and services.

In retrospect, it's clear that haphazard technology integration never worked well.

The resurgence of the U.S. companies was rooted in a new approach to R&D. During the 1960s and 1970s, U.S. companies such as IBM, Xerox, and AT&T succeeded by making breakthrough discoveries in their R&D laboratories and then turning those inventions into breakthrough products. The names of their R&D operations—the Thomas J. Watson Research Center, the Palo Alto Research Center, and Bell Laboratories—became synonymous with U.S. innovativeness.

Technology integration, such as it was, occurred in the following manner: isolated research groups would explore new technologies and choose which ones the development organization would use; the development organization would refine them; and the new product or process would then be passed on to a manufacturing organization, which would remove the bugs. Because there was no process for taking a view of the entire project when choosing technologies, many of the choices were poor. That outcome is not surprising, considering the traditional roles of scientific research (exploring the potential of narrowly defined technological possibilities) and of development (turning a specified set of technologies into detailed designs and manufacturing processes).

In retrospect, it is clear that this haphazard approach to technology integration never worked well. But its shortcomings did not become glaringly apparent until the competitive landscape changed during the 1980s. Mere tinkering wouldn't suffice. U.S. computer companies needed something new to bridge the gap between research and development—to turn outstanding research into outstanding products and processes. Traditional industrial labs could not fill the role. They had been developed to shield research organizations from day-to-day business pressures so that researchers could focus on creating or discovering important technological concepts.

The U.S. companies that prevailed in the computer industry in the 1990s abandoned the traditional R&D

model and created a radically new one. They did not stop conducting basic research, but they did shift much of the focus of their research efforts to applied science, and they turned to an increasingly diverse base of suppliers and partners—universities, consortia, and other companies—to help generate technological possibilities. In addition, they formed tightly knit teams of expert integrators—people with extensive backgrounds in research, development, and manufacturing—to develop new generations of major products and processes. Those integrators were given various titles—process integrators at Intel, program managers at Microsoft—but they all carried out similar functions. Companies charged the integration teams to take a broad, systemwide outlook and gave them considerable freedom in conceptualizing the new generation and choosing its technologies. The aim was for the teams to create a concept of the future product that would fit customers' requirements and could be manufactured rapidly and efficiently. They were thus given overall responsibility for developing the concept, and they worked closely with developers to deliver a perfected product and production process to manufacturing. Developers and, in many instances, suppliers had responsibility for individual components, but the integration team retained responsibility for the whole project. In addition, companies gave the integration teams enormous resources for testing a wide range of technological possibilities. The result was an approach to technology integration that excelled in finding important new technologies that provided extremely successful solutions and in finding them very quickly and efficiently. (See the exhibit "The Emergent Model of R&D in the U.S. Computer Industry.")

The Emergent Model of R&D in the U.S. Computer Industry

1. Internal and external research organizations generate a variety of technological options.

2. The integration team investigates, selects, and refines the options, making use of extensive experimental facilities.

3. The team works with developers to deliver a complete generation of a product or process.

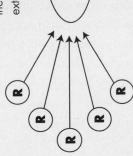

Solutions
Products
Processes

The approach took advantage of local conditions, such as the employee churn that had become a way of life in many U.S. industries. It exploited the country's wealth of top-notch research universities and the ready supply of people with graduate degrees that they produced. Instead of keeping teams intact from project to project, the companies refreshed them for each new generation of a product or process by bringing in people who were conducting cutting-edge research at universities and other businesses.

This model would be difficult to deploy in Japan. Because the country has a much weaker tradition of university research, Japanese companies cannot access the rapidly evolving base of fundamental knowledge in science and engineering through universities the way U.S. companies can. And because long-term employment—at least at large companies—is the norm, Japanese companies cannot obtain knowledge by luring away competitors' employees.

Japanese integrators tend to favor incremental improvements or refinements of familiar technologies.

They must develop most of their fundamental knowledge internally or obtain it from suppliers or alliances with U.S. companies. But Japanese companies do enjoy certain advantages: close links with suppliers, strong cross-functional relationships among employees, and a wealth of employees who have been involved in creating several generations of a product or process.

To choose which technologies to employ, Japanese companies rely on a network of veteran employees—few of whom have Ph.D.'s—who work in a variety of functions. A loosely structured group of about a dozen people usually coordinates the effort, but its role does not resemble that of the intense, centrally located, dedicated U.S. integration teams.

In addition, the network of integrators at a Japanese company does not usually have anywhere near the resources for experimentation that the U.S. integration teams enjoy. To select technologies, integrators rely on a collective intuition that is rooted in their experience in previous projects. They then test possible technologies in a relatively small number of carefully selected experiments. Compared with the U.S. approach, the Japanese approach tends to result in the choice of a higher proportion of evolutionary technologies. Japanese integrators are less likely to employ cutting-edge technologies; they tend to favor incremental improvements on or refinements of technologies with which they are already familiar.

The point of the above comparisons is not to suggest that one approach is better than another. Rather, it is to say that an effective organization can construct an approach to technology integration that suits its national culture and assets. The recent history of the semiconductor industry offers a striking example. Over the past four years, we accumulated extensive data on more than 30 semiconductor development projects conducted by U.S., Japanese, and Korean companies. The data document how various approaches can be effective.

The U.S. Comeback in Semiconductor R&D

In the 1960s and 1970s, U.S. companies first invented semiconductors and then dominated the market. AT&T's Bell Laboratories was responsible for numerous innovations, including the transistor and electron-beam lithography. IBM was the first company to develop a truly high-volume semiconductor production process for transistor-based solid-logic technology, introduced in 1964. Texas Instruments later perfected high-volume semiconductor production. And U.S. companies such as Fairchild and Intel were the first to introduce most of the designs for widely used logic and memory chips.

The 1980s, however, witnessed the rise of powerful new semiconductor manufacturers in Asia. A group of Japanese companies led by Hitachi, NEC, and Toshiba gained a substantial advantage by developing new production technology and investing heavily in technology-integration and manufacturing capabilities. Korean scientists and engineers trained largely in the United States returned home with the latest knowledge in lithography, etching, and transistor design and helped build the base in fundamental science and technology that Korea needed to become a player in the industry. A group of Korean companies headed by Samsung achieved market share leadership in DRAMs by the early 1990s.

Meanwhile, U.S. and European companies fell years behind in the development of production-process technology, which put them at a tremendous disadvantage, particularly in the DRAM business, where most of the profits are made the year after a new generation of process technology is introduced. Prices for a generation of DRAMs fall rapidly after the first supplies hit the market; a six-month delay can make the difference between enormous profits and heavy losses. By the early 1980s, Japanese manufacturers were already in the lead in DRAMs, and Samsung was gaining ground. IBM, Texas Instruments,

Inadequate investment in manufacturing capacity was not to blame for the decline of the U.S. semiconductor industry.

and Intel introduced the 256K DRAM generation more than a year and a half behind Hitachi, the leader. And they were more than two years behind in introducing the next generation of DRAMs: 1-megabit chips.

By the late 1980s, the U.S. semiconductor industry seemed doomed. Japanese companies dominated product development and manufacturing. Their market share increased from 26% in 1980 to 49% in 1990; in memory devices it jumped from 22% to 70%. Intel, National, Advanced Micro Devices (AMD), Motorola, AT&T, and Mostek withdrew from the manufacture of DRAMs, and many industry experts predicted that Japanese competitors would soon threaten Intel's position in microprocessors. Total employment in the U.S. companies, including their overseas operations, dropped by more than 25,000 between 1983 and 1990, despite the fact that global semiconductor sales more than tripled during the 1980s.

When asked about the root causes of these failures, many academics and business executives cite a lack of investment in manufacturing capacity resulting from the short-term focus of U.S. corporations and Wall Street. When we analyzed development projects in detail, however, we discovered that capital expenditures and the size of investments in R&D were not the culprits. In fact, we discovered that delays had occurred long before massive manufacturing investments were necessary. Because of poor technological choices in DRAM architecture and process design made early in the game, the U.S. companies' chips were physically bigger and, consequently, more expensive than the offerings of their Japanese and Korean rivals. Faced with the prospect of investing massive amounts of money in a process that would get them to the market late with an inferior product, U.S. managers, not surprisingly, declined to do so.

But U.S. manufacturers that remained in the business performed a seemingly impossible feat: they turned themselves around. Their revival is captured in the graph "A Comparison of Process-Development Performance in DRAMs," which shows that the non-Japanese companies that decided to remain in the business—mainly U.S. and Korean companies—dramatically improved their performance. The graph focuses on the most critical measure of integrated circuit performance: its density. A difference of 1 on the graph corresponds to an advantage of about a year and a half in the introduction of comparable products. A value greater than 1 indicates a performance that is higher than the average; a value less than 1 indicates inferior performance.

The figure shows a very substantial performance gap between Japan and the rest of the world in the 64-kilobit through the 1-megabit generations. At its maximum, the average gap between the introduction of comparable products by Japanese companies and by their competitors was more than two years. But then the gap narrowed in the 4-megabit generation and disappeared with the 16-megabit and 64-megabit generations. The Japanese organizations had shorter lead times and greater circuit density in the generations completed in the mid and late 1980s, but this advantage completely evaporated in the 1990s. Additionally, the graph shows that for the last generation, the averages of both Japanese and non-Japanese companies were considerably above the industry's long-term trend line. The trend line is based on data from all generations, so this performance indicates that the remaining competitors became faster. The survivors in the business had raised the average rate of technological progress.

The graph "A Comparison of Process-Development Performance in Microprocessors" shows a similar improvement trajectory in logic chips. In this case, a difference of 1 on the graph corresponds to an advantage of slightly more than two and a half years in the introduction of comparable products. We divided the U.S. competitors into two groups. The first, composed of IBM

A Comparison of Process-Development Performance in DRAMs

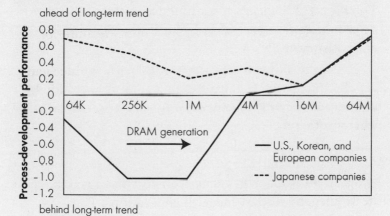

In this graph, and in "A Comparison of Process-Development Performance in Microprocessors," we have kept the industry's trend line constant; in actuality, it increases sharply. More formally, the graphs display the normalized residuals from regressions of the logarithm of transistor density against time. A value of 1.0 indicates that the group of projects is one standard deviation ahead of the long-term trend. A value of -1.0 shows that the group of projects is one standard deviation behind the trend. To compare performance in DRAMs, we aggregated the data for non-Japanese companies, including U.S., Korean, and European manufacturers. Plotting U.S. and Korean averages separately does not change the basic picture.

and Intel, dramatically increased its performance; the second, which includes weaker players, continued to lag and tried unsuccessfully to compensate for inferior process technology with more aggressive chip designs.

But by the mid-1990s, members of the second group had to resort to mergers and alliances in order to survive. AMD merged with NexGen, which had access to IBM's process expertise through an alliance. Similarly, Cyrix, Motorola, and Hewlett-Packard decided to enter into alliances and subcontract most of their process R&D and high-volume microprocessor manufacturing—the first two companies to IBM and the third to Intel. Of the less efficient U.S. group, only DEC remained as a truly independent competitor by 1996. The message once again: companies that do not introduce new generations of a production process early cannot survive.

A Comparison of Process-Development Performance in Microprocessors

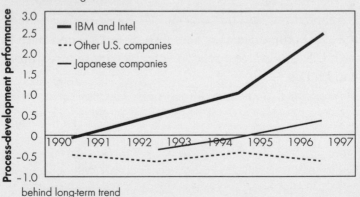

The Evidence

Improvements in performance by U.S., Japanese, and Korean semiconductor companies did not stem from such sources as increased research or scientific breakthroughs. Discovering new technologies was not enough. Successful companies were those most adept at choosing technologies that would work together in an increasingly complex production system. (See "The Evolving Challenge of Semiconductor Development" at the end of this article.)

In the United States, companies had to rethink their technology integration processes. The ultimately successful U.S. organizations abandoned the step-by-step model of R&D, created dedicated integration teams, and shrank the role their research and manufacturing organizations played in choosing technologies.

Our data show that the foundation of the U.S. semiconductor industry's turnaround differed from the foundations on which Japanese and Korean industries built their successes. (See the table "Integration Teams in the Semiconductor Industry.") An explicit or de facto policy of long-term employment prevailed at the Japanese and Korean companies but was almost completely absent at the U.S. companies. Our data also show that compared with U.S. integrators, relatively few Japanese integrators had Ph.D.'s.

We found that the Korean companies had adopted an intermediate model. Although long-term employment was generally the norm, many project participants had been hired from other companies, mostly from the United States. A higher percentage of Ph.D.'s were hired than in the Japanese projects—approaching 50% at some Korean companies. Interestingly, U.S. universities had awarded many of the Ph.D.'s. In contrast to the Japanese group, therefore, Korean companies were able to absorb significant external sources of knowledge—primarily from the United States.

Because of differences in employment practices, the proportion of people in projects who had experience developing previous generations of products and processes was much higher at the Japanese and Korean companies than it was at the U.S. companies. Not coincidentally, the Japanese and Korean companies also invested more in training and developing the individuals involved in projects than their U.S. competitors did. Instead, the U.S. companies hired people from universities to provide the specific expertise needed to tackle

A tremendous capacity for experimentation allowed U.S. teams to investigate many technologies simultaneously.

Integration Teams in the Semiconductor Industry: The Career Dynamics and Experience of Their Members

	U.S.	Japan	Korea
Percentage with explicit or de facto long-term employment guarantees	14	100	100
Percentage with research experience in Ph.D. programs	59	7	24
Percentage with no previous R&D project experience	34	14	14
Percentage with experience in one project	28	34	22
Percentage with experience in two projects	23	30	23
Percentage with experience in more than two projects	15	23	41

immediate tasks and to achieve specific objectives in their R&D programs. For example, U.S. companies often recruited people from Stanford University to obtain expertise in computer simulation and from the Massachusetts Institute of Technology for expertise in lithography.

The different backgrounds of project members influenced the processes that companies used to generate knowledge in their R&D projects. (See the table "Experimentation Capacity Available to Integration Teams in DRAM and Microprocessor Projects.") The Japanese and Korean companies relied intensely on employees who had worked on previous generations of a production process. They confirmed the intuition of these experienced project members by conducting a relatively small number of experiments. In sharp contrast, the U.S. companies relied heavily on knowledge brought in by newcomers. Although their concepts offered the potential for great performance improvements, the innovations had to be tested thoroughly before they could be

---

Experimentation Capacity Available to Integration Teams in DRAM and Microprocessor Projects

	U.S.	Japan	Korea
Experimentation capacity *(wafers that can be produced per week)*	1,450	480	417
Average experimental iteration time *(average number of weeks required to manufacture an experimental sample)*	16	13	6
Minimum experimental iteration time *(minimum number of weeks required to manufacture an experimental sample)*	5	7	5

A high capacity for experimentation allows a team to test a broad range of technological possibilities. A low average-iteration time allows for rapid feedback from each experiment. A low minimum-iteration time allows for rapid bursts of experimentation.

adopted, which explains why the U.S. projects had much greater experimentation capacity than the Japanese or Korean projects.

In the early 1990s, U.S. companies *tripled* the amount of fabrication capacity that their integration teams could use. (See the chart "The Growth of Experimentation Capacity in the Semiconductor Industry.") By 1993, the U.S. integrators possessed on average more than twice the experimental capacity of their Japanese counterparts. This capacity enabled the U.S. teams to investigate a variety of technological options simultaneously. In semiconductor development, scientists and engineers test ideas by fabricating experimental circuits. Such tests require many steps and extremely expensive equipment, including so-called clean rooms for fabricating silicon wafers. In addition, the U.S. teams' ability to use fully functional equipment permitted them to simulate the final manufacturing facility accurately, which is the main reason the role of their manufacturing departments in the overall R&D process declined.

The Growth of Experimentation Capacity in the Semiconductor Industry

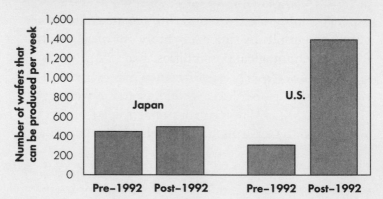

We also found differences in the typical organization of R&D. In the United States, projects were highly centralized. Once the integration team had made its technological choices, it worked with development and production specialists to refine the new manufacturing process until it was fully operational and generated high yields. Only then did the team transfer responsibility for the production process to manufacturing.

In contrast, a network of several functions and suppliers carried out R&D in the Korean and Japanese companies. Research and manufacturing shared much more of the decision-making responsibility at the project level. A small group of technology integrators usually led the selection process for the entire production system and was responsible for its successful implementation. But the group did not actually perform the ramp-up; instead, it handed off the process to manufacturing when the yields were still relatively low. The average yield at the time of transfer in the U.S. projects (58%) was markedly higher than the average in the Japanese projects (21%) or the Korean projects (25%).

All three models resulted in effective integration, but in different ways. Generally, the Japanese projects achieved high performance (faster, smaller, and less expensive integrated circuits) through an evolutionary path—essentially by squeezing more out of relatively mature technological possibilities. The U.S. projects tended to achieve high performance in a more revolutionary fashion—by the early adoption of novel, aggressive technologies. The Korean projects apparently achieved high performance through a hybrid approach. Our methodology allowed us to analyze to what extent the performance of a product was linked to *fundamental* improvements in technology, such as changes in line width. This analysis showed that U.S. companies, on average, made fundamental changes earlier than their Japanese competitors. Although we did not conduct the same level of field research in Korea that we did in the United States and Japan, the data suggest that Korean companies were in between. (See the exhibit "Revolutionary and Evolutionary R&D Projects.")

Leveraging Research Capability

Technology integration alone does not explain the stunning rise of Japanese and Korean companies and the dramatic turnaround of U.S. semiconductor manufacturers. The recovery of the U.S. companies, for example, would never have been possible without the solid foundation of scientific discoveries made at industrial laboratories and universities during the 1980s and 1990s. That said, without effective technology-integration processes—processes tailored to the local culture and conditions—the U.S. companies would not have been able to take advantage of that foundation.

Leveraging research foundations is critical in a variety of industries. Internet software and semiconductor manufacturing don't have much in common; nor do pharmaceuticals and advanced materials. But all those environments share common challenges: a *novel* base of technology and a *complex* context in which that technology must be applied. That combination of novelty and complexity makes a company's excellence in technology integration critical. Not surprisingly, some of the most successful U.S. companies in such industries take a similar approach: they recruit people at the cutting edge of their scientific and engineering disciplines and give

Revolutionary and Evolutionary R&D Projects

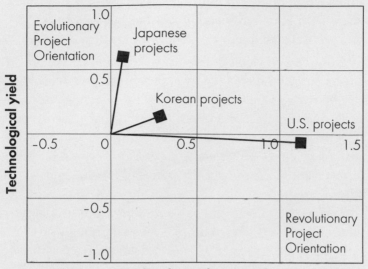

Technological potential

Technological potential measures whether the fundamental technologies included in the project are ahead of or behind the industry's long-term trend, and is derived from a physical model of circuit performance applied to DRAMs and microprocessors introduced between 1990 and 1995. Projects above the trend use novel technologies; those below the trend use refinements of existing technologies. Technological yield measures how much potential is realized in actual product performance. A value of 1.0 in each measure indicates that the project is one standard deviation ahead of the long-term trend. A value of -1.0 shows that the project is one standard deviation behind.

The graph shows that U.S. projects, on average, exhibit high technological potential and relatively low yield, indicating that they are ahead of the trend in the application of novel technologies. Japanese projects achieve relatively low potential and high yield, indicating that they are more evolutionary in character, squeezing performance out of more conservative technologies. Korean projects are in between.

The overall project performance is the sum of the two axes, which shows that U.S. projects for these generations of DRAMs and microprocessors slightly outperform the Japanese and Korean projects.

them enormous resources to test a wide range of technological options. In workstations, the integration and development teams at Silicon Graphics had the resources to simulate possible designs and validate concepts acquired from universities and other companies. Microsoft's and Netscape's software-development processes hinge on hiring highly experienced people from competitors and universities, building system prototypes daily, and frequent beta testing. In pharmaceuticals, Eli Lilly recently invested heavily in combinatorial chemistry techniques, which allow its world-class researchers to test rapidly the therapeutic effectiveness of millions of new compounds.[2]

The results of our study also highlight the subtlety inherent in the design of an effective technology-integration process. An R&D organization resides in a given geographic environment, and its effectiveness is linked to its ability to leverage local expertise, customs, and traditions. An approach that requires a person to accumulate experience in generations of development projects may not be appropriate in Silicon Valley, where the turnover in critical employees can easily exceed 20% per year. Similarly, an approach that depends on transferring innovative technologies from universities may work only if those institutions are nearby or if there is a long-standing relationship between a company and an academic institution.

Our findings underline the point that the unique research base of the United States—its rich network of universities and industrial laboratories—is a national asset that the private and public sectors should protect and expand. And it is an asset that U.S. companies must strive to leverage. By designing processes that integrate this research base with existing and emerging markets,

U.S. companies can position themselves and the nation to excel in an increasingly complex technological future.

The Evolving Challenge of Semiconductor Development

DURING THE 1980S AND 1990S, the nature of semi-conductor process development changed fundamentally, and companies found themselves needing new approaches to R&D. Every 18 months, more and more transistors had to be included on a single circuit. In 1964, Gordon Moore, who cofounded Intel in 1968, predicted that integrated circuit density would double every year. His prediction, which became known as Moore's Law, proved remarkably accurate. In 1996, commercially available integrated circuits included more than 6 million transistors.

To achieve such densities, semiconductor developers have had to cope with increasingly complex products and manufacturing processes. The maximum number of interconnects on a logic chip is expected to soar from about 60 in 1992 to 2,000 in 2007; the number of gates is expected to grow from 900,000 in 1992 to 100 million; and the number of metal layers is expected to increase from about three to more than six. The number of steps required to manufacture such devices doubled between 1980 and 1990. It tripled between 1990 and 1995, and it is expected to triple again before 2001.

To deal with a development challenge of this magnitude, researchers and engineers must contend with a growing number of variables in each new generation. More production steps must be defined and tested; more components must be checked and combined. Each new production step increases the risk of expensive manufacturing failures. More steps, therefore, raise the standard that must be achieved at each step. Achieving a very modest yield of 75% from even a 50-step production process requires that each step perform at a yield of 99.4%; that is, no more than 6 of every 1,000 chips can be defective at each step.

In addition to this complexity, companies also have had to contend with the increasing pace of technological innovation. During the 1990s, developers pushed into such fields as plasma etching and deep-ultraviolet and X-ray lithography, in which the underlying physics were poorly defined at best. At this frontier, researchers could not predict exactly where or when physical limits to existing processes would be reached. Therefore, they could not predict precisely which problems a given development program would run into. Very often, technical options were not clearly defined at the outset of a program, and important technology was not yet proven. Developers were confronted by ill-defined problems and a confusing variety of potential solutions, which could come from anywhere on the globe.

As technological complexity and novelty have grown, the consequences of technical failure have become potentially catastrophic. The cost of a minimum-size factory to manufacture memory chips, for example, increased from about $4 million in 1971 to more than $1.2 billion in 1996. Most of the additional expense for production facilities is the cost of fabrication equipment: about 85% of the cost of a new semiconductor plant is equipment. By 2001, the cost is projected to climb to more than $4 billion.

The real challenge has been to figure out which options to choose from the palette of available technologies in order to find a solution that can be developed smoothly and that will function coherently. In the early days of the semiconductor industry, it was relatively simple to guess which technologies would yield performance improvements. A few bright engineers could take a stab at the likely technological solutions and then tweak the system so that it delivered the desired levels of performance. In the 1980s, this informal approach ran out of gas. Choosing the technologies that can function best in the future manufacturing environment has become the essence of semiconductor development.

Notes

1. Our study, which began in 1990, so far includes 87 development projects conducted by more than 30 companies. We studied 33 projects that were developing semiconductor technologies, 15 in high-performance workstations, 27 in mainframes, and 12 in software.
2. Stefan H. Thomke, Eric A. von Hippel, and Roland R. Franke discuss this methodology in detail in "Modes of Experimentation: An Innovation Process Variable," Harvard Business School Working Paper 97-052.

Originally published in May–June 1997
Reprint 97304

When Is Virtual Virtuous?

Organizing for Innovation

HENRY W. CHESBROUGH AND
DAVID J. TEECE

Executive Summary

CHAMPIONS OF VIRTUAL CORPORATIONs are urging
managers to subcontract anything and everything.
Because a number of high-profile corporate giants have
been outperformed by more nimble, "Networked"
competitors, the idea of the virtual organization is tantalizing. But is virtual really the best way to organize for
innovation?

Henry W. Chesbrough and David J. Teece argue
that the virtual corporation has been oversold. Innovation is not monolithic, and it is critically important to
understand the type of innovation in question. For some
innovations, joint ventures, alliances, and outsourcing
can play a useful role. But for others, they are inappro-
priate—and strategically dangerous. The initial success—
and subsequent failure—of the IBM PC illustrate the
strategic mistake of using virtual approach for the kind of

complex technology that should have been controlled in-house.

The authors present a framework to help managers determine when to innovate by going virtual, when to form alliances, and when to rely on internal development. They proved a range of cases to illustrate how to match organizational strategy to the type of innovation being pursued. General Motors, for example, used the wrong approach to develop disk brake technology and paid the price: getting to market later than its competitors. To realize its vision of "tetherless communication," Motorola must choose and organizational strategy allowing it more control over the direction and timing of technological change than a virtual approach could provide. In contrast, the virtues of the virtual organization are illustrated by Ameritech's use of alliances to influence the innovation path in multimedia.

CHAMPIONS OF VIRTUAL CORPORATIONS are urging managers to subcontract anything and everything. All over the world, companies are jumping on the bandwagon, decentralizing, downsizing, and forging alliances to pursue innovation. Why is the idea of the virtual organization so tantalizing? Because we have come to believe that bureaucracy is bad and flexibility is good. And so it follows that a company that invests in as little as possible will be more responsive to a changing marketplace and more likely to attain global competitive advantage.

There is no question that many large and cumbersome organizations have been outperformed by smaller "networked" competitors. Consider the eclipse of IBM in

PCs and of DEC in workstations by Packard Bell and Sun Microsystems. But while there are many successful virtual companies, there are even more failures that don't make the headlines. After many years of studying the relationship between organization and innovation, we believe that the virtues of being virtual have been oversold. The new conventional wisdom ignores the distinctive role that large integrated companies can play in the innovation process. Those rushing to form alliances instead of nurturing and guarding their own capabilities may be risking their future.

What's Special about Virtual?

What gives the virtual company its advantage? In essence, incentives and responsiveness. Virtual companies coordinate much of their business through the marketplace, where free agents come together to buy and sell one another's goods and services; thus virtual companies can harness the power of market forces to develop, manufacture, market, distribute, and support their offerings in ways that fully integrated companies can't duplicate. As William Joy, vice president of research and development at Sun Microsystems, puts it,

The incentives that make a virtual company powerful also leave it vulnerable.

"Not all the smart people [in the workstation industry] work for Sun." Because an outside developer of workstation software can obtain greater rewards by selling software to Sun customers than by developing the same software as a Sun employee, he or she will move faster, work harder, and take more risks. Using high-powered, market-based incentives such as stock options and attractive bonuses, a virtual company can quickly access the technical resources it needs, if those resources are available. In situations where technology is changing rapidly, large companies that attempt to do everything inside will flounder when competing against small companies with highly trained and motivated employees.

But the incentives that make a virtual company powerful also leave it vulnerable. As incentives become greater and risk taking increases, coordination among parties through the marketplace becomes more and more difficult, precisely because so much personal reward is at stake. Each party to joint development activity necessarily acts in its own self-interest. Over time, innovation can generate unforeseen surprises that work to the advantage of some parties and to the disadvantage of others. The result: Once-friendly partners may be unwilling or unable to align strategically, and coordinated development activity falters. In contrast, integrated, centralized companies do not generally reward people for taking risks, but they do have established processes for settling conflicts and coordinating all the activities necessary for innovation.

This trade-off between incentives and control lies at the heart of the decision that managers must make about how to organize for innovation. (See the graph "Finding the Right Degree of Centralization.") If virtual organizations and integrated companies are at opposite ends of the spectrum, alliances occupy a kind of organizational middle ground. An alliance can achieve some of the coordination of an integrated company, but, like players in a virtual network, the members of an alliance will be driven to enhance their own positions, and over time their interests may diverge. The challenge for managers is to choose the organizational form that best matches the type of innovation they are pursuing.

Types of Innovation

When should companies organize for innovation by using decentralized (or virtual) approaches, and when should they rely on internal organization? The answer depends on the innovation in question.

Some innovations are *autonomous*—that is, they can be pursued independently from other innovations. A new turbocharger to increase horsepower in an automobile engine, for example, can be developed without a

---

Finding the Right Degree of Centralization

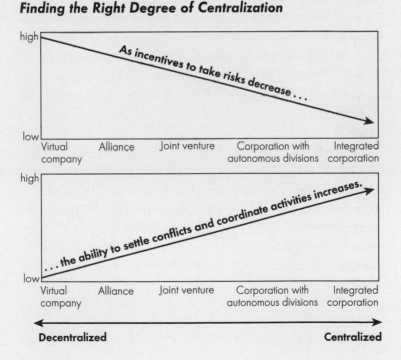

complete redesign of the engine or the rest of the car. In contrast, some innovations are fundamentally *systemic*—that is, their benefits can be realized only in conjunction with related, complementary innovations. To profit from instant photography, Polaroid needed to develop both new film technology and new camera technology. Similarly, lean manufacturing is a systemic innovation because it requires interrelated changes in product design, supplier management, information technology, and so on.

The distinction between autonomous and systemic innovation is fundamental to the choice of organizational design. When innovation is autonomous, the decentralized virtual organization can manage the development and commercialization tasks quite well. When innovation is systemic, members of a virtual organization are dependent on the other members, over whom they have no control. In either case, the wrong organizational choice can be costly.

Consider what happened to General Motors when the automobile industry shifted from drum brakes to disc brakes, an autonomous innovation. General Motors was slow to adopt disc brakes because it had integrated vertically in the production of the old technology. GM's more decentralized competitors relied instead on market relationships with their suppliers—and the high-powered incentives inherent in those relationships. As a result, they were able to beat GM to market with the new disc brakes, which car buyers wanted. When companies inappropriately use centralized approaches to manage autonomous innovations, as GM did in this case, small companies and more decentralized large companies will usually outperform them.

To understand why the two types of innovation call for different organizational strategies, consider the information flow essential to innovation. Information about new products and technologies often develops over time as managers absorb new research findings, the results of early product experiments, and initial customer feedback. To commercialize an innovation profitably, a tremendous amount of knowledge from industry players, from customers, and sometimes from scientists must be gathered and understood. This task is easier if the information is codified.

Codified information—for example, specifications that are captured in industry standards and design rules—can often be transferred almost as effectively from one company to another as it can within a single company. Because such information is easily duplicated, it has little natural protection. Sometimes bits and pieces can be protected by intellectual property rights, but those pieces, especially trade secrets and patents, are small islands in a broad ocean of knowledge.

Other information does not travel as easily between companies. Tacit knowledge is knowledge that is implicitly grasped or used but has not been fully articulated, such as the know-how of a master craftsman or the ingrained perspectives of a specific company or work unit. Because such knowledge is deeply embedded in individuals or companies, it tends to diffuse slowly and only with effort and the transfer of people. Established companies can protect the tacit knowledge they hold, sharing only codified information. They can be quite strategic about what they disclose and when they disclose it.

The information needed to integrate an autonomous innovation with existing technologies is usually well understood and may even be codified in industry standards. Systemic innovations, on the other hand, pose a unique set of management challenges regarding information exchange. By their very nature, systemic innovations require information sharing and coordinated adjustment *throughout an entire product system.* Here is where a market-based, virtual approach to innovation poses serious strategic hazards. Unaffiliated companies linked through arm's-length contracts often cannot achieve sufficient coordination. Each company wants the other to do more, while each is also looking for ways to realize the most gain from the innovation. Information sharing can be reduced or biased, as each seeks to get the most at the other's expense. In most cases, the open exchange of information that fuels systemic innovation will be easier and safer within a company than across company boundaries. The inevitable conflicts and choices that arise as a systemic innovation develops can best be resolved by an integrated company's internal management processes.

The Case of Industry Standards

Coordinating a systemic innovation is particularly difficult when industry standards do not exist and must be pioneered. In such instances, virtual organizations are likely to run into strategic problems. Consider how technical standards emerge. Market participants weigh many competing technologies and eventually rally around one of them. There are winners and losers among the contestants, and potential losers can try to undermine the front-runner or to fragment the standard by promoting a rival. Until a clear winner emerges, customers may choose to sit on the sidelines rather than risk making the wrong choice.

By virtue of its size and scope, an integrated company may be able to advance a new standard simply by choosing to adopt a particular technology. If a large company commits itself to one of a host of competing technologies, consumers as well as companies promoting rival technologies will probably be persuaded to follow suit. Virtual companies, however, which may be struggling to resolve conflicts within their networks, won't be able to break a deadlock in a complicated standards battle. Players in a network won't be able to coordinate themselves to act like a large company.

Once a new standard has been established, virtual organizations can manage further innovation quite well. But when an industry begins to advance technology to a new level, the cycle can begin anew. Again, technically feasible choices present new strategic trade-offs. Suppliers, competitors, and customers may fail to agree on a common path. Unless a big player emerges to break the logjam among rival technologies, the existing standard will prevail long past its usefulness.

Today computer floppy disks are frozen in an old standard because no single company has been able to establish a new one. IBM pioneered the 3.5-inch hard-case diskette in 1987 when it introduced its new line of PS/2 personal computers. Within two years, the memory capacity of 3.5-inch diskettes doubled from 720 kilobytes to 1.44 megabytes, where it has remained ever since.

Why? The technical capability to expand diskette capacity is available, but no company has the reputation and strength to set a new standard. Through the 1980s, IBM was large enough to coordinate standards among the key participants in the industry: personal computer manufacturers, diskette makers, and software publishers. If IBM told the industry it would use a particular capacity on its next generation of machines, others did the same. But in the 1990s, IBM's leadership of the PC market came to an end, perhaps permanently. Today IBM is not strong enough to move the industry by itself, and it won't move ahead of the other industry players and risk being stranded if they don't follow.

A simple rule of thumb applies: When innovation depends on a series of interdependent innovations— that is, when innovation is systemic—independent companies will not usually be able to coordinate themselves to knit those innovations together. Scale, integration, and market leadership may be required to establish and then to advance standards in an industry.

The IBM PC: Virtual Success or Failure?

IBM's development of the personal computer is a fascinating example of both the advantages and disadvantages of using virtual approaches to pursue innovation. When IBM launched its first PC in 1981, the company elected to outsource all the major components from the marketplace. By tapping the capabilities of other companies, IBM was able to get its first product to market in only 15 months.

More than a few analysts hailed IBM's development of the PC as a new business model.

The microprocessor (the 8088) was purchased from Intel, and the operating system (which became PC-DOS) was licensed from a then fledgling software company, Microsoft. In effect, the IBM PC had an "open" architecture: It was based on standards and components that were widely available. The high-powered incentives of the marketplace could coordinate the roles of component manufacturers and software vendors. IBM successfully promoted its open architecture to hundreds of third-party developers of software applications and hardware accessory products, knowing that those products would add to the appeal of the PC.

IBM also relied on the market to distribute the product. Although IBM launched its own IBM Product Centers as retail storefronts and had its own direct sales force for large corporate customers, the majority of the company's systems were distributed through independent retailers, initially ComputerLand and Sears. Eventually, there were more than 2,000 retail outlets.

By using outside parties for hardware, software, and distribution, IBM greatly reduced its investment in bringing the PC to market. More important, those relationships allowed IBM to launch an attack against Apple, which had pioneered the market and was growing quickly. The IBM PC was an early success, and it spawned what became the dominant architecture of the entire microcomputer industry. By 1984, three years after the introduction of the

IBM's virtual approach prevented the company from directing the PC architecture it had created.

PC, IBM replaced Apple as the number one supplier of microcomputers, with 26% of the PC business. By 1985, IBM's share had grown to 41%. Many observers attributed the PC's success to IBM's creative use of outside relationships. More than a few business analysts hailed the IBM PC development as a model for doing business in the future.

Indeed, IBM's approach in its PC business is exactly the kind of decentralized strategy that commentators are urging large, slow-moving companies to adopt. The early years of the IBM PC show many of the benefits of using markets and outside companies to coordinate innovation: fast development of technology and tremendous technological improvements from a wide variety of sources.

With the passage of time, though, the downside of IBM's decentralized approach has become apparent. IBM failed to anticipate that its virtual and open approach would prevent the company from directing the PC architecture it had created. The open architecture and the autonomy of its vendors invited design mutinies and the entry of IBM-compatible PC manufacturers. At first, competitors struggled to achieve compatibility with IBM's architecture, but after several years compatibility was widespread in the industry. And once that happened, manufacturers could purchase the same CPU from Intel and the same operating system from Microsoft, run the same application software (from Lotus, Microsoft, WordPerfect, and others), and sell through the same distribution channels (such as ComputerLand, BusinessLand, and MicroAge). IBM had little left on which to establish a competitive advantage.

To maintain technological leadership, IBM decided to advance the PC architecture. To do that, IBM needed to coordinate the many interrelated pieces of the architecture—a systemic technology coordination task. However, the third-party hardware and software suppliers that had helped establish the original architecture did not follow IBM's lead. When IBM introduced its OS/2 operating system, the company could not stop Microsoft from introducing Windows, an application that works with the old DOS operating system, thereby greatly reducing the advantages of switching to OS/2. And third-party hardware and software companies made investments that extended the usefulness of the original PC architecture. Similarly, Intel helped Compaq steal a march on IBM in 1986, when Compaq introduced the first PC based on Intel's 80386 microprocessor, an enhancement over the earlier generations of microprocessors used in IBM and compatible machines. Even though IBM owned 12% of Intel at the time, it couldn't prevent Intel from working with Compaq to beat IBM to market. This was the beginning of the end of IBM's ability to direct the evolution of PC architecture.

By the third quarter of 1995, IBM's share of the PC market had fallen to just 7.3%, trailing Compaq's 10.5% share. Today its PC business is rumored to be modestly profitable at best. Most of the profits from the PC architecture have migrated upstream to the supplier of the microprocessor (Intel) and the operating system (Microsoft), and to outside makers of application software. The combined market value of those suppliers and third parties today greatly exceeds IBM's.

IBM's experience in the PC market illustrates the strategic importance of organization in the pursuit of innovation. Virtual approaches encounter serious problems when companies seek to exploit systemic innovation. Key development activities that depend on one another must be conducted in-house to capture the rewards from long-term R&D investments. Without directed coordination, the necessary complementary innovations required to leverage a new technology may not be forthcoming.

The Virtuous Virtuals

How have the most successful virtual companies accomplished the difficult task of coordination? The virtual companies that have demonstrated staying power are all at the center of a network that they use to leverage their own capabilities. Few virtual companies that have survived and prospered have outsourced everything. Rather, the virtuous virtuals have carefully nurtured and guarded the internal capabilities that provide the essential underpinnings of competitive advantage. And they invest considerable resources to maintain and extend their core competencies internally. Indeed, without these companies' unique competencies and capabilities, their strategic position in the network would be short-lived.

Consider the well-known battle between MIPS Technologies and Sun Microsystems for control of workstation processors. (See Benjamin Gomes-Casseres, "Group Versus Group: How Alliance Networks Compete," HBR July-August 1994.) MIPS was trying to promote its Advanced Computing Environment (ACE) against Sun's Scalable Processor Architecture (SPARC). Sun had strong internal capabilities, whereas MIPS tried to compete as a more virtual player, leveraging off of the

Nike relies on Asian partners for manufacturing, but its design and marketing capabilities allow it to call all the shots.

competencies of partners such as Compaq, DEC, and Silicon Graphics. MIPS had a good technical design, but that was literally all it had, and this hollowness left the company at the mercy of its partners. As soon as DEC and Compaq reduced their commitment to the ACE initiative, the network fell apart and pulled MIPS down with it. The very reliance of virtual companies on partners, suppliers, and other outside companies exposes them to strategic hazards. Put another way, there are plenty of small, dynamic companies that have not been able to outperform larger competitors. In particular, a hollow company like MIPS is ill equipped to coordinate a network of companies. Although Sun also worked with alliance partners, it had strong internal capabilities in systems design, manufacturing, marketing, sales, service, and support. As a result, Sun can direct and advance the SPARC architecture, a dominant technology in the industry.

Many companies with superior capabilities have prospered as the dominant player in a network. Japanese keiretsu are structured that way. Consider Toyota, whose successful introduction of the lean production system—a truly systemic innovation—required tremendous coordination with its network of suppliers. Because Toyota was much larger than its suppliers, and because, until recently, it was the largest customer of virtually all of them, it could compel those suppliers to make radical changes in their business practices. In a more egalitarian network, suppliers can demand a large share of the economic benefits of innovations, using what economists call hold-up strategies. Strong central players like Toyota are rarely vulnerable to such tactics and are thus in a better position to drive and coordinate systemic innovation.

The most successful virtual companies sit at the center of networks that are far from egalitarian. Nike may rely on Asian partners for manufacturing, but its capabilities in design and marketing allow it to call all the shots. In the computer industry, Intel has effective control of the 80×86 microprocessor standard, Microsoft dominates PC operating systems, and Sun is driving the SPARC architecture. Those companies control and coordinate the advance of technologies in their areas, and in this regard they function more like integrated companies than like market-based virtuals.

Choosing the Right Organizational Design

Today few companies can afford to develop internally all the technologies that might provide an advantage in the future. In every company we studied, we found a mix of approaches: Some technologies were "purchased" from other companies; others were acquired through licenses, partnerships, and alliances; and still other critical technologies were developed internally. Getting the right balance is crucial, as IBM's disastrous experience in PCs illustrates. But what constitutes the right balance? (See "Ameritech's Strategy for Emerging Technologies" at the end of this article.)

Consider how a successful innovator such as Motorola evaluates the trade-offs. Motorola, a leader in wireless communications technology, has declared its long-term goal to be the delivery of "untethered communication"—namely, communication anytime, anywhere, without the need for wires, power cords, or other constraints. In order to achieve that goal, Motorola must make important decisions about where and how to advance the required technologies. Those decisions turn on a handful of questions: Is the technology systemic or likely to become systemic in the future? What capabilities exist in-house and in the current supplier base? When will needed technologies become available?

For Motorola, battery technology is critical because it determines the functionality that can be built into a handheld communications device and the length of time that the device can be used before recharging. Batteries have been a pacing technology in this area for many years.

As Motorola scans the horizon for improved battery technology, it encounters a familiar trade-off between the degree of technological advancement and the number of reliable volume suppliers. Conventional battery technologies such as nickel cadmium (Ni-Cd) have become commodities, and there are many suppliers. But few if any suppliers can offer the more advanced technologies Motorola needs. And the most exotic technologies, such as fuel cells and solid-state energy sources, are not yet commercially viable from any supplier. How should Motorola organize to obtain each of the technologies it might need? Under what circumstances should the company buy the technology from a supplier and when should it form alliances or joint ventures? When should Motorola commit to internal development of the technology? (See the matrix "Matching Organization to Innovation.")

For Ni-Cd technology, the clear choice for Motorola is to buy the technology, or to use the market to coordinate access to this technology, because Motorola can rely on competition among many qualified suppliers to deliver what it wants, when needed, for a competitive price. Motorola faces a more complex decision for fuel cells and solid-state battery technologies. Should Motorola wait until those technologies are more widely available, or should the company opt for a joint venture or internal development?

Before deciding to wait for cutting-edge battery technologies to be developed, Motorola must consider three issues. One is that Motorola could lose the ability to influence the direction of the technology; the early commercial forms may be designed for applications that do not benefit Motorola, such as electric automobiles. The second problem is that Motorola might lose the ability to pace the technology, to bring it to market at a competitively desirable time. The third issue is that if such technologies are—or become—systemic and Motorola has no control over them, the company may not be able to advance related technologies and design features to achieve its goal of untethered communication.

Matching Organization to Innovation

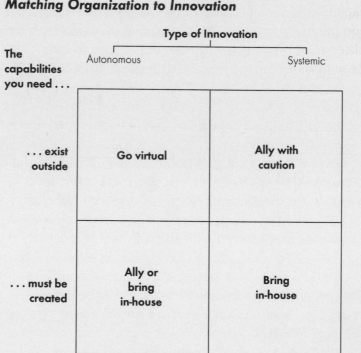

Those issues suggest that Motorola cannot simply wait for the technologies to be provided by the market. Rather, Motorola needs to build strong ties to suppliers with the best capabilities, thus increasing its ability to direct the path of future systemic innovation. Where Motorola itself has strong capabilities, the company should pursue the technologies on its own.

To retain its leadership over the long term, Motorola must continue to develop the critical parts of its value chain internally and acquire less critical technologies from the market or from alliances. Although networks with their high-powered incentives may be effective over the short term for an unchanging technology, they will not adapt well over the long term as technology develops and companies must depend on certain internal capabilities to keep up. The popularity of networked companies and decentralization arises, in part, from observations over a time horizon that is far too short. Remember the enthusiasm that greeted IBM's early success in PCs.

Scale and Scope

Business history presents us with a lesson of striking relevance to the organizational decisions managers face today. In the classic *Scale and Scope*, Alfred Chandler details how the modern corporation evolved in the United States, Germany, and Great Britain at the end of the nineteenth century. Managers who invested the capital to build large-scale enterprises blazed the trail for the leading industries of the second industrial revolution. Markets in railroads, steel, chemicals, and petroleum were developed and shaped by major companies, not the other way around. The most successful of those companies were the first in their industries to make the massive investments in manufacturing, management, and distribution that were needed to realize the gains from innovation.

Companies that failed to make such coordinated, internal commitments during this period were soon thrust aside. The experience of British companies provides a cautionary tale for the champions of the virtual company. Many enjoyed early technological leads in their industries, but the reluctance of those family-run companies to relinquish control to outside investors prevented them from investing to build the capabilities they needed to commercialize their technologies. When German or U.S. competitors made the requisite investments, British companies lost their leadership position. In chemicals, for example, the British lead in the 1870s was completely lost by 1890. History even provided British chemical companies with a second chance when Germany's defeat in World War I temporarily cost German chemical manufacturers their plants and distribution networks. But by 1930, German chemical companies regained the lead because the British again failed to invest adequately. The lesson is that companies that develop their own capabilities can outperform those that rely too heavily on coordination through markets and alliances to build their businesses.

The leading industries of the late nineteenth and early twentieth centuries—chemicals, steel, and railroads—all experienced rapid systemic innovation. The winners were the companies that made major internal investments to shape the markets, rather than those that relied on others to lead the way. While business

conditions have certainly changed, many of the principles that worked a century ago still pertain.

Today leading companies like Intel and Microsoft
make extensive investments to enhance their current
capabilities and spur the creation of new ones. Because
so many important innovations are systemic, decentralization without strategic leverage and coordination is
exactly the wrong organizational strategy. In most cases,
only a large company will have the scale and scope to
coordinate complementary innovations. For both the
chemicals industry 100 years ago and the microcomputer industry today, long-term success requires considerable and sustained internal investment within a
company. The lessons of the second industrial revolution apply to the third: Adept, well-managed companies
that commit the right internal resources to innovation
will shape the markets and build the new industries of
the twenty-first century.

Ameritech's Strategy for Emerging Technologies

AMERITECH, a Regional Bell Operating Company with
wire and fiber assets in the Midwest, has the potential to
be a major player in the development of on-demand
video and interactive information services for home use. In
emerging technologies such as multimedia, no one has all
the information to determine what capabilities a company
must develop internally or access through the market. The
only certainty is that the promise of this market will
depend on the co-development of many technologies,

including data formats, throughput rates, wiring topologies, billing systems, and user interfaces.

Because the eventual configuration of the multimedia industry is unknown (and arguably unknowable ex ante), organizations such as Ameritech must become insiders to the discussions among a range of potential industry players. In emerging markets that are dependent on evolving technologies, considerable information sharing among a wide variety of companies will ultimately result in a road map for the industry. Virtual organizations can serve as catalysts to the development of industry directions and standards in ways that fully integrated organizations cannot.

Consider the role of alliances in Ameritech's multimedia strategy. By allying its own capabilities with those of companies with relevant and complementary skills, Ameritech can participate directly in defining and developing an architecture that will ultimately manage the emerging technologies. One such alliance is with Random House, a leading print publisher of books and magazines, with properties such as the *New Yorker*, Condé Nast, Fodor's, and Arthur Frommer Travel Guides. Random House is capable of supplying significant "content" over Ameritech's wires into the home. This alliance allows both companies to begin to explore the business and technical requirements of providing content into the home.

Ameritech and Random House have formed a joint venture to acquire a start-up virtual company called Worldview Systems, which publishes an electronic monthly current-events database of travel information about more than 170 destinations around the world. While Worldview Systems' products are now sold primarily through travel agents and an 800 telephone number, Ameritech and Random House believe that this type of product may turn out to be ideal for delivery to the home. As Thomas Touton, Ameritech Development's vice president for venture capital, notes, such exploratory investments "require support from senior management willing to move fast in investing but be patient in waiting for returns, and an investment focus that is strongly synergistic with the company's operations."

When and if the promise of the multimedia market becomes real, Ameritech will doubtless be competing against other powerful players. But Ameritech may already have an inside track in the race to deliver information and video on demand into the home. Through alliances such as the one with Random House and exploratory investments in virtual companies such as Worldview Systems, Ameritech has been able to share information and know-how with other potential industry participants and become an insider with the potential to influence the direction of this nascent industry. Until a technological direction becomes clear, companies must invest in capabilities and become active participants in the information dissemination process. Virtual organizations can be an extremely valuable tool at this early stage of market evolution.

Originally published in January–February 1996
Reprint 96103

The New Logic of
High-Tech R&D

GARY P. PISANO AND
STEVEN C. WHEELWRIGHT

Executive Summary

FEW MANAGERS OF high-technology companies view
manufacturing as a primary source of competitive advantage. Indeed, companies in high-tech industries increasingly outsource manufacturing completely. In so doing,
they hope to avoid the risks of investing in expensive
manufacturing plants and losing sight of what they see
as their true source of advantage: product research and
development.

The authors' research in the health care industry over
the past decade suggests that such thinking is often
costly and potentially dangerous to the competitive
health of high-tech companies. In fact, it is not only possible but also necessary to excel at developing new products and new manufacturing processes simultaneously. In
many high-tech markets in which product technology is
rapidly evolving, manufacturing process innovation is

becoming an increasingly critical capability for product innovation.

Companies that have treated process development as an integral part of product development have accrued tremendous advantages. The authors' discovery of a record of success by certain drug companies that have achieved such integration should catch the attention of executives in other high-tech industries. Process development might be more important in their industries than many managers realize.

FEW MANAGERS OF HIGH-TECHNOLOGY companies view manufacturing as a primary source of competitive advantage. Indeed, a trend in an increasing number of high-tech industries is for companies to outsource manufacturing completely to third-party contractors or joint-venture partners. In so doing, those companies hope to avoid the risks of investing in expensive manufacturing plants and losing sight of what they see as their true source of advantage: product research and development.

Our research in the health care industry over the past decade, including a recently completed study of the pharmaceutical industry, suggests that such thinking is often costly and potentially dangerous to the competitive health of high-tech companies. In fact, it is not only possible to excel at simultaneously developing new products and new manufacturing processes but also necessary. In many high-tech markets in which product technology is rapidly evolving, manufacturing-process innovation is becoming an increasingly critical capability for product innovation. This trend means that many companies should devote more resources and attention to process R&D.

Consider the following example: Sigma Pharmaceuticals (a fictitious name for a real company) spent ten years and more than $100 million researching, developing, and clinically testing a new drug to treat a serious infectious disease. By all accounts, the project was a smashing success. Clinical trials demonstrated that the drug was safe and highly effective, and it quickly won the approval of the U.S. Food and Drug Administration (FDA) for commercial marketing. Unfortunately, senior managers were so focused on making sure that the product moved through clinical trials as quickly as possible that they gave the process-development side of the project short shrift.

Making the drug, which consisted of a complex molecule, required the development of breakthrough process technology. Senior managers, however, did not allocate significant resources to process development until they were confident that the drug would receive FDA approval. By that point, it was too late for Sigma to increase the yields of the process technology before it began to sell the drug. As a result, the company could not meet initial demand without major investments in additional capacity—a task that took nearly two years to complete. In the meantime, the company lost potential sales. Even worse, it lost its opportunity to penetrate the market while it had an exclusive position. (The FDA is expected to approve a competing drug shortly.)

Manufacturing-process innovation is more and more critical to product innovation.

Sigma's predicament was not the result of poor forecasting: During the lengthy process of clinical trials, the company collected ample data on the toxicity and efficacy of the drug—all of which made it possible to predict the likely demand. Nor was Sigma's predicament the result of wild-eyed scientists creating an unmanufacturable product and then throwing it over the wall to an unsuspecting manufacturing group: The people charged with developing the process technology were experienced, first-rate scientists who worked closely with the manufacturing group, running their pilot production tests in the plant and effecting a smooth transfer to full-scale manufacturing. Rather, Sigma's inability to ramp up production quickly and the relatively low yields of its manufacturing process were the consequence of its underinvesting in process development, particularly in the early stages of the product-development cycle.

And Sigma is far from an exception. In our recently completed study of 23 major development projects at 11 U.S. and European pharmaceutical companies, we saw many instances in which problems in developing the process either delayed a product launch or inhibited the commercial success of the product once on the market. [1] The root cause of those failures was, more often than not, senior managers' belief that process technology was not very important. Much to our surprise, we found managers with that attitude not only at established drug companies but also at young biotech companies. We have witnessed the same phenomenon in a variety of other high-tech industries. Because successful products commanded significant price premiums and because manufacturing costs were small relative to revenues, executives failed to view, nurture, and manage manufacturing technologies as a strategic capability.

We also have observed the tremendous advantages that some companies in a variety of high-tech industries have accrued by treating process development as an integral part of the product-development cycle. For example, a handful of drug companies had managers who deliberately built organizational capabilities that supported fast, efficient, and effective process development. With their new capabilities, the companies could introduce new products more quickly, with high yields and controlled processes that gave them a significant cost advantage over competitors. They then further strengthened their positions by continuing to pursue process improvements aggressively after the launch of new products. As a result, they were able to launch their new products more smoothly, commercialize complex products more easily, and penetrate markets more rapidly than before. And, strikingly, they often required less capital investment and fewer overall development resources than their more conventional competitors. Our discovery of this pattern in pharmaceuticals—an industry in which product innovation is paramount— should give executives in other high-tech industries pause: Process development might be more important in their industries than they think.

The Hidden Leverage of Process Technology

When asked why they have decided not to make process development and process innovation a priority, executives in many high-tech industries typically respond that the benefit of such a focus is lower manufacturing costs, which is not particularly important to them. But those executives are ignoring other considerable benefits generated by process development. These include accelerated time-to-market for new products, rapid production ramp-up, enhanced product functionality, and a stronger proprietary position.

ACCELERATED TIME-TO-MARKET

In many more situations than is generally imagined, the development of manufacturing technology heavily influences new product introductions. One drug company had just come to this realization when we studied it.

Rapid ramp-up and accelerated time-to-market are only two of the many benefits of focusing on process development.

Eager to shorten the time required to develop and win FDA approval for new products and to leverage existing development spending, senior executives, in typical industry fashion, had devoted the vast majority of the company's R&D spending to product innovation. But managers within the process-development organization admitted that the time required to develop process technologies and to prepare factories for production generally added a year to product-development lead times. Tellingly, senior management was unaware of that problem.

Process development also can influence product-development lead times in more subtle ways. For example, in businesses such as pharmaceuticals and semiconductors, some process development generally needs to take place before functional prototypes or representative product samples can be fabricated; slow process development at this stage can cause long lead times for prototypes, which, in turn, can delay the introduction of the product. Delays also can occur if the process technology developed early on is incapable of producing sufficient quantities of test materials. Even worse, when a poorly understood and out-of-control process technology results in prototypes whose quality is low or erratic, test results may be inaccurate or unreliable. In biotechnology, new molecules are so complex to manufacture that developing basic process technology often determines the lead times for commencing human clinical testing. (Ironically, despite the widespread recognition of the difficulty of manufacturing biotechnology-based drugs, many executives in the industry often think that leading-edge science only takes place in product research.)

In addition, low-yielding processes often make it impossible for a company to produce enough material to supply all the necessary clinical trials in a timely fashion. When that occurs, companies have no choice but to delay or extend the clinical-trial schedule, which ultimately results in commercialization delays. At one company, we asked a group of managers involved in a particular project whether process development had delayed the timing of clinical trials. Simultaneously, the director of process development said no and the person overseeing clinical development said yes. It turned out that both were right. Process development succeeded in supplying enough material to support the clinical-trial schedule for one specific application of the drug. However, as is true for most drugs, there were multiple potential therapeutic applications. Because the process yields were relatively low, the company could not produce enough of the drug to support the other clinical trials with its existing capacity, and thus those trials were delayed.

RAPID RAMP-UP

When a new product is introduced into the factory, it can take some time for manufacturing performance (in terms of costs; the productivity of labor, equipment, and capital; capacity; quality; and yields) to reach normal long-term levels. This period is generally known as the ramp-up. To a large degree, ramp-up speed is a function of the quality of the process technology, which, in turn, is determined by process development.

Rapid ramp-up is invaluable for several reasons: The faster a company can ramp up production of a new product, the more quickly it can begin to earn significant revenues from the new product and recoup its development investments. Rapid ramp-up enables a company to penetrate the market quickly, gain broad market acceptance, and begin to accumulate experience with high-volume production. And, finally, the faster ramp-up occurs, the faster critical resources can be freed to support the next development project. In contrast, when companies launch a new product with process technologies that are poorly understood and riddled with bugs, they use a good deal of their manufacturing capacity producing scrap and must spend a significant portion of their scarce engineering resources solving production problems rather than producing more new products.

At one company in our study, problems starting up a new process technology for a major new product were so great that the company reassigned every scientist and engineer from process development to the project. Eventually, the process worked well enough for the product to be launched. But the launch was six months later than scheduled and well over budget; and the cost of manufacturing the product was still too high, forcing the company to invest additional resources into improving the process technology. What is more, the massive dedication of process-development resources to this project deprived other projects of the resources they needed. As a result, those projects were at risk of experiencing serious problems later on in the start-up phase.

ENHANCED PRODUCT FUNCTIONALITY AND CUSTOMER ACCEPTANCE

Most end users do not care about the process that is used to make a product. Yet, in many contexts, those features of the product that they do care about—such as consistency, purity, size, weight, reliability, and environmental impact—are directly determined by the specifics of the production process. Those specifics are largely dependent on the application of superior process capability early in the product-development process. In pharmaceuticals, even minor

Innovative process technologies that are protected by patents or that are difficult to duplicate can block or stymie a would-be imitator's push into the market.

changes in the chemical-production or biochemical-production process can alter the characteristics of a product, affecting its therapeutic properties. The link between process technology and product characteristics is particularly tight in biotechnology. Slight changes in the genetics of cells used in the production process, reaction conditions, or purification processes can make the difference between having a product that is safe and therapeutically active and having one that is not.

EXTENDED PROPRIETARY POSITION

Innovative process technologies are an underexploited way for organizations to protect and extend the proprietary position of their products. Great new products are two-edged swords. They create new markets, attract buyers willing to pay premium prices, and enable a company to generate significant profits. The better and more successful the product, however, the more competitors strive to imitate it. And imitators can be swift and ruthless. Companies have traditionally fended off imitators with patents, but patents rarely provide complete protection. Even when they do, long lead times between the discovery of the patentable technology and its commercialization may mean that such protection expires relatively early in the product's commercial life. But innovative process technologies that are protected by patents or that are difficult to duplicate can block or stymie a would-be imitator's push into the market. (It is easier to stay ahead of a competitor that must constantly struggle to manufacture the product at competitive cost and quality levels.) Some pharmaceutical companies have learned that when a drug's patent expires, proprietary process technology is one of the best protections against intrusion by generic manufacturers.

Driving Forces: The Changing Face of High-Technology Settings

Managers are well aware that shorter product life cycles, increasingly hard-to-manufacture product designs, fragmented markets, and growing technological parity are changing the nature of competition in many high-tech industries. Although that fact is no revelation, many managers are only beginning to understand how these forces have elevated the strategic value of the process-development capabilities that we just discussed.

Shorter product life cycles. A ubiquitous force in global high-technology competition is the relentless shortening of product life cycles. Ironically, managers of some high-tech companies use shorter life cycles as a reason to eschew in-house manufacturing and to concentrate on product R&D. Apparently, they see process technology and manufacturing assets as albatrosses in a world where rapid product changes can make plants and equipment obsolete overnight. However, the shrinking of product life cycles also elevates the importance of fast time-to-market and rapid ramp-up. Indeed, it is increasingly essential to develop manufacturing processes that have relatively low capital-investment requirements and relatively high capital productivity at the *start* of commercial production, and that therefore offer short payback horizons. Semiconductor fabrication facilities, for instance, which can cost more than $1 billion and have useful economic lives of just a few years, incur millions of dollars in depreciation charges weekly; it is for reasons like these that yield improvement and rapid ramp-up play such a critical role in semiconductor manufacturing.

The strategy of commencing commercial production with poorly developed or unstable processes and improving them over time is too costly. Even in cases in which some portion of the production investment can be carried over to the next product generation, shorter product life cycles are making the capability to develop highly efficient processes before a product launch—and to improve them aggressively thereafter—a strategic imperative.

Increasingly hard-to-manufacture product designs.
It was once thought that a key to successful product development was to separate invention from development; that is, a company should use only proven technologies in its new product development. In rapidly changing markets (such as high-performance workstations, flat panel displays, and semiconductors), such a conservative approach is no longer viable. To gain even a temporary edge in product performance or functionality, companies must work at the frontiers of technology and, in industries such as biotechnology or advanced materials, at the frontiers of science. For some types of technologies, this imperative creates significant challenges and uncertainty for process development and manufacturing. The costs of developing and implementing new process technologies often approach and sometimes greatly exceed the costs of product development. Although every organization should find ways to avoid unnecessary complexity, those with strong process-development and manufacturing capabilities will have more freedom in developing products than those forced to stick with simple-to-manufacture designs.

Fragmented, demanding markets. Customers for both high-tech and low-tech products—whether they are end users, distribution channels, industrial users, or health care institutions—are now demanding flexibility, service, and customized features. Such increasingly demanding and fragmented markets add to the product-development challenge. They require manufacturing processes that can respond to the need for a variety of customized features, services, and product forms without degrading quality, adding cost, or slowing delivery. When such manufacturing processes are developed proactively, they can better satisfy these demanding requirements and provide significant, enduring positions in new segments. Consider McNeil Consumer Products' gel-cap version of Tylenol. A distinctive manufacturing process provided an easy-to-swallow product; and because the process was proprietary, the product was the only one in its class with that feature. As a result, the gel cap strengthened Tylenol as a brand.

Growing technological parity. During the 1960s, many U.S. high-tech companies were able to dominate world markets on the basis of their prowess in product technology. Today the situation is vastly different. Geographic origin is no longer a significant barrier to gaining access to basic technology. Companies cannot afford to ignore any area—including manufacturing technology—in pursuing a competitive advantage.

Indeed, companies of any nationality can locate their R&D facilities in any particular region to tap its technological expertise. For example, Japanese electronics companies have R&D facilities in Silicon Valley; U.S. electronics companies have established design centers in Japan; and European pharmaceutical companies conduct a significant amount of their R&D in the United States. Companies also can gain access to state-of-the-art technology through collaborative relationships with other companies or universities. A highly mobile scientific and engineering labor force and relatively weak intellectual-property protections are additional factors encouraging the rapid diffusion of technological knowhow and competencies across countries and companies.

But because manufacturing processes take place behind factory walls, manufacturing technologies often are harder to imitate than product technologies and therefore offer a more sustainable source of competitive advantage.

Lessons from Pharmaceuticals

Over the past several years, the pharmaceutical industry has grappled with a number of wrenching changes. In many cases, these changes have been driven by industry-specific versions of the forces cited above—shorter product life cycles, increasingly hard-to-manufacture products, fragmented and demanding markets, and growing product-technology parity. In coping with these changes, a few companies have made process development a priority. Often at odds with conventional wisdom and past business practices, these approaches offer companies in a wide range of industries a way to create a sustainable advantage in today's high-technology environment. (See "How Manufacturing Can Make Low-Tech Products High-Tech" at the end of this article.)

Throughout the 1960s, 1970s, and 1980s, five basic practices characterized process development at pharmaceutical companies: When developing a new drug, delay significant process R&D expenditures until there is reasonable certainty that the product will be approved for commercial launch; process R&D is successful when it stays off the critical path for the launch of the new product; once a product is on the market and demand begins to grow, the primary task of manufacturing and process engineering is to bring on-line additional physical capacity; whenever possible, locate manufacturing in a tax

haven, even if it is far from R&D and process development; consider investments in process improvements
later in the patent life of a product when the threat of
generic competition becomes imminent. These practices
appeared to be based on sound logic and an irrefutable
set of principles: Don't waste resources on products that
will never come to market; don't delay product launch;
don't stock out of a high-margin product; do minimize
taxes and maximize after-tax earnings; and do extend
the product life where possible. The rationale was com-
pelling. Product development in pharmaceuticals has
always been a highly uncertain endeavor. Only about 5%
of the new compounds that make it to human clinical
testing ultimately reach the market. And by some
accounts, only one out of every 10,000 new compounds
discovered in the laboratory ultimately become commercial drugs. Until the 1990s, the vast majority of drugs
were relatively simple to manufacture, which meant that
process development, in turn, involved relatively few
major technical challenges. In addition, it could be completed relatively quickly, so companies could afford to
wait until late in the development cycle to start it. And
with manufacturing costs often amounting to less than
10% of revenues, even grossly inefficient processes had
little impact on a company's competitive position or
financial results.

Companies also have had limited discretion in changing their manufacturing processes without consulting
the FDA. If a process change is significant enough, the
FDA may require the company to conduct additional
human clinical trials to prove that the new manufacturing process has not changed the safety or efficacy profile
of the drug. As a result, once a drug hits the market,

companies have preferred to add capacity by duplicating an existing process rather than by aggressively improving process technologies.

Although specific practices in pharmaceuticals may be unique to the industry, similar patterns of behavior arise in other industries. For example, at most companies, developing products at the frontiers of technology, concerns about the technical feasibility of product designs and about whether markets will actually materialize as expected tend to overshadow concerns about manufacturing. There is a natural tendency to postpone dealing with process technology and manufacturing issues, which seem issues far off in the future. (And, if the product fails, will never be issues at all.) If a product does reach the market and demand takes off, then there is little time to think about developing new or improved process technology. The goal at this stage is to produce as much as you can as fast as you can. Adding physical capacity and finding outsourcing partners become expedient strategies. If the product cannot be imitated easily by competitors and its value to the customer is high, margins may be high enough for such a strategy to work.

Pharmaceutical companies find themselves squeezed by shorter product life cycles, less pricing flexibility, and higher costs.

By almost any measure, the set of practices that pharmaceutical companies pursued worked for many years. Until recently, the industry was one of the most profitable and fastest-growing sectors of the U.S. economy. From 1982 to 1992, the industry's average annual growth rate was 18%. Throughout the 1970s and 1980s, the average pharmaceutical company's earnings and return on equity grew at a double-digit pace, fueled by a host of new products, strong patent protection, and pricing flexibility. Traditionally, average gross margins on products ranged from 70% to 85% in the United States and from 60% to 70% in Europe.

Today, however, pharmaceutical companies find themselves squeezed by shorter product life cycles, less pricing flexibility, and higher costs. The result: a dramatic recasting of the opportunities for growth and profits. (See the chart "The Margin Squeeze in the Pharmaceutical Industry.")

Shorter periods of exclusivity and less pricing flexibility. Traditionally, pharmaceutical companies made money by launching blockbuster drugs and maintaining an exclusive position until the patent expired. Rivalry within most therapeutic classes was relatively limited.

The Margin Squeeze in the Pharmaceutical Industry

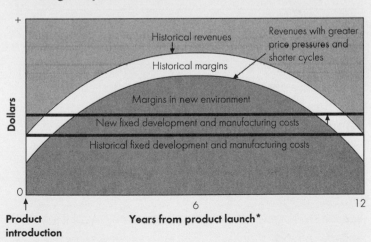

*Note: These numbers are approximations based on a typical drug.

Even as growth in product volumes slowed and the number of new product approvals declined in the late 1980s, profits continued to grow through price increases.[2]

Recently, however, the rapid expansion of health maintenance organizations and other managed care networks has concentrated drug purchasing and vastly increased buyers' bargaining power. Because they buy drugs in huge quantities and often limit purchases to only one or two drugs for a given condition, these networks can successfully press for price discounts as deep as 60%.

Competition also has increased significantly. By 1993, roughly half of all prescriptions in the United States were filled with generics, up from about 2% in 1980.[3] These generic products are typically priced 30% to 60% below competing brand-name products. Between 1993 and 1999, patents on branded drugs with annual sales of $20 billion will expire, and generic substitutes are expected to capture a significant share of these sales thereafter. In addition, an overwhelming majority of the drugs on the market currently face direct competition from other patented drugs for treating the same diseases. As one senior executive noted, "Nowadays, everybody is playing in the same sandbox." As a result, companies often not only have less time before generics enter the market but also face competition from patented alternatives even before their own patents expire. Additionally, a company's patent-protected drug can face stiff price competition if a low-priced generic version of a competitor's drug whose patent has expired enters the market.

Escalating costs of development and manufacturing. Because of increasing regulatory requirements and the complexity of new compounds, the cost of developing a new drug increased to $359 million in 1992 (taking into account the cost of the many compounds that never made it to market), up from $120 million five years ear-lier.[4] The cost of manufac-turing these pharmaceuti-cals also is increasing. In the early 1990s, manufac-turing costs represented about 20% of sales, up from 10% in the early 1980s.[5] At 20% of sales,

To achieve unique cost structures, compromises must focus on creating distinctive sets of manufacturing capabilities.

manufacturing costs on average now exceed R&D costs. Because the cost of manufacturing generic products is typically 50% to 70% of revenues and because generics' share of the market is expected to climb rapidly during the next several years, it is quite likely that the cost of goods sold relative to revenues will become even greater for the pharmaceutical industry as a whole.

Why are manufacturing costs escalating? Relatively stringent FDA regulations on product quality require drug companies to invest in more sophisticated produc-tion equipment and controls. Environmental Protection Agency regulations force them to invest in costly pollu-tion-control equipment and waste-treatment facilities. Although advances in drug discovery and design technology have enabled drug researchers to synthesize more complex (and possibly safer and more effective) molecules in the laboratory, large-scale manufacturing of these complex molecules typically requires more advanced and costly production technology. Today com-panies may have to spend $100 million to $400 million on new facilities to produce active chemical ingredients for a single drug—approximately double the amount they had to spend ten years ago.

The challenge facing drug companies (and other high-tech companies in similar environments) is far more complex than shifting their emphasis from product innovation to lower costs. Although the pharmaceutical industry continues to be a business in which new product innovation is paramount, how a company manages process development will influence to a significant degree the extent to which it can dramatically lower its manufacturing

How a company manages process development will greatly determine its success in product innovation and in lowering manufacturing costs.

costs and continue to excel at product innovation. In many instances, companies will have to create new strategies, approaches, and organizational capabilities to enable process development to contribute fully to the product-development process.

Creating a New Manufacturing Cost Structure

The challenge of dramatically reducing manufacturing costs has led many drug companies to streamline their plant networks and outsource a larger fraction of their production. Given the history of excess production capacity at many companies and the haphazard plant networks that have evolved over years of political and tax-driven strategies, these structural changes should yield significant benefits. However, if everyone restructures, everyone will reap roughly the same benefits and no one will achieve a distinctive advantage. In order to achieve new cost structures that are difficult to imitate, companies must focus on creating distinctive sets of manufacturing capabilities. Process development is the primary means for creating those capabilities.

Like companies in other industries, most pharmaceutical companies have relied on the gradual buildup of knowledge to lower their manufacturing costs over time. Indeed, the effects of cumulative experience on costs can be very powerful. However, real leverage comes from an aggressive pursuit of process-technology changes rather than a simple focus on operating existing technology better to increase volume and boost capacity utilization. The lower curve in the chart "Impact of Process Development on Cost Improvement" shows the effects of 12 years of manufacturing experience on the costs of producing a typical antibiotic. As indicated, manufacturing costs fell by approximately 85% during this period. The company conducted more than 80 projects on the manufacturing process, about half of which were relatively minor (such as fine-tuning equipment and improving operating procedures). The other half were major process-improvement projects requiring significant capital expenditures and engineering resources (such as improving equipment designs and altering the basic chemistry of the process). The chart compares what the learning curve actually looked like with what it would have looked like had the company conducted no further process development after launching the product.

One of the most striking results of the process improvements at this company was a reduction in the capital that had to be invested to meet demand. The chart "How Process Development Reduces Capital Costs" compares the number of reactor vessels (each costing around $7 million) required to meet demand versus the number that would have been needed without any process-driven productivity improvements. The numbers are staggering: To meet demand in 1994, the company actually needed 17 reactors with a replacement cost of $119 million. Had no process development been undertaken and had process yields not improved dramatically, the company would have needed closer to 120 reactors. Somewhere along the line, the company would have had to invest more than $700 million of additional capital to support this product.

So much for conventional wisdom, which holds that waiting as long as possible to make investments in process development is the best policy! Our findings show that the effects of process development are cumulative—the earlier a company undertakes process development, the greater the total financial return. Conversely, the longer a company waits to initiate process development, the less incentive there is to do so: Once a

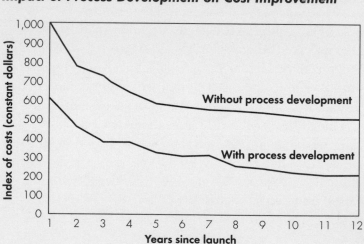

Impact of Process Development on Cost Improvement

How Process Development Reduces Capital Costs

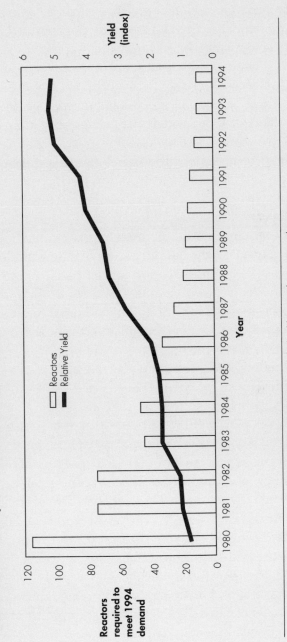

Note: Bars refer to the number of reactors required to meet 1994 demands had yields stopped improving in that year.

company builds sufficient physical capacity to meet peak demand, the yield improvements generated by process development will lead to excess capacity.

If it is beneficial to conduct process development early in the commercial life of a product, it is even better to do it well before a product is launched. Our findings fly in the face of two widely held views: that it is best to avoid investing scarce technical resources in a project that may never make it to market and that it is best to keep process development from interfering with the launch schedule. The data presented in "How Process Development Reduces Capital Costs" suggest that investing in process development earlier could have a major impact on the cost structure of a new product. Whereas the traditional approach emphasizes moving down the learning curve in later years, our findings show that process development conducted prior to commercial launch results in getting on a better (lower-cost) learning curve at the outset.

When minimal prelaunch process work results in underdeveloped, problem-riddled, inefficient process technologies, the chances are that the postlaunch process-development effort will be nothing more than Band-Aid fixes that leave little time (if any) for proactive improvement initiatives. In the pharmaceutical industry, as in many other industries, a poor process can be improved only so much. There are usually several possible synthetic routes for making most traditional chemical-based drug. Identifying the best route—in other words, the best sequence of chemical reactions that produce the sought-after molecule—in the early stages of developing a drug is the key to obtaining a manufacturing process capable of high yields and rapid throughput. One company in our study found that its choice of synthetic route determined 70% of a product's total manufacturing costs on average. Developing a high-performing process sooner rather than later is especially important for a biotechnology company, because, as we mentioned earlier, when such a company makes even minor changes in a process, the FDA typically requires it to conduct additional clinical studies to demonstrate that the changes have not altered the drug's therapeutic properties.

Achieving Rapid Process Development before Launch

On projects of comparable scope and complexity, our data revealed significant differences in how quickly individual companies could complete process development. In many of the projects in our sample that had excessive lead times, technical problems emerged late in the development cycle and made the process unfit for commercial use. Many of these problems were caught only when attempts were made to make the process technology operational on a commercial scale. Simply put, the quality of the process development was inadequate.

Just as it is costly and time consuming to let a product with a quality problem make it through the factory and into the customer's hands, it is costly and time consuming to rectify process-design problems on the factory floor. High-quality process development that finds and eliminates process-design problems early in the development cycle—rather than throwing armies of scientists and engineers at a project later—is the key to shortening process-development lead times. In our research, we identified a handful of practices that drug companies use to achieve this result.

What goes on *before* a technology transfer is more important than what goes on *during* the transfer. Everyone recognizes the futility of transferring technology by "throwing it over the wall." As a consequence, when projects experience problems in this phase, they are immediately assumed to be rooted in the transfer procedures. For example, we heard manufacturing managers complain about such problems as not seeing the technology until the last minute, not getting enough support from R&D during the transfer phase, and receiving incomplete descriptions. Meetings were called. Task forces were formed. Consultants were brought in. And reforms were implemented, including better documentation, clear rules for when a technology was ready to be transferred, specific sign-off points, and the establishment of joint-technology transfer teams. Such steps probably do help improve communications between the people who develop the process and those who will be using it in the plant. But our research suggests that the source of most problems arising during the transfer phase have little to do with communication; rather, they are rooted in the process technology itself and how it has been developed.

Ultimately, any process technology must perform under actual manufacturing conditions. We saw many instances in which processes performed well under laboratory conditions but could not meet commercial objectives when run on full-scale production equipment using ordinary production workers and standard operating procedures. These problems were not the result of poor technology transfers but of poor process development.

Use pilot production as an in-line quality-control check. Undertaking quality checks throughout all phases of a development project can generate substantial benefits. In developing a new drug, pharmaceutical companies subject chemical compounds to a series of clinical performance tests. Interestingly, when it comes to developing process technologies, they often do not engage in the same rigorous quality checks. Instead, companies allow problems to percolate until they finally emerge during the start-up of commercial production. The problems will be caught, but only after it becomes costly and time-consuming to fix them.

Pilot production can be a very effective way to test knowledge and assumptions about a process design before full-scale commercial production. Every company we studied engaged in pilot production, yet we observed very different approaches to using it. Some companies viewed pilot production's role as simply producing enough materials so that the appropriate tests of the product (including clinical trials) could be conducted. In these companies, processes were transferred to the pilot-production facility when sufficient quantities of material could no longer be made in the laboratory. In some other cases, when other products were utilizing the pilot facility fully, test batches were produced in laboratory facilities.

A distinct minority of the companies we studied, however, took an alternative learning-driven approach. The companies viewed pilot production as integral to the discovery and resolution of process-design problems. They tended to start pilot production when they felt sufficient learning had occurred in a laboratory setting and they needed to test the process design in a setting more representative of the future plant environment.

Development speed is determined by what you do early in the life of the project. To the surprise of many managers, we found that total spending on process development did not influence process-development lead times, but the timing and focus of such spending did. For instance, in the projects for developing chemical-based pharmaceuticals that we studied, we found a correlation between intense exploration and analysis of alternative processes in the laboratory at an early stage and more rapid process development. (See the exhibit "Impact of Process Research on Process-Development Lead Times.") The reason is straightforward: Chemical-process technology rests on a very mature knowledge base. Valid theories, engineering rules of thumb, and practical experience help process developers use laboratory results to identify and anticipate many potential production problems. These results can then be quickly validated in a pilot plant.

It is not clear, however, what the optimal approach for reducing lead times in biotechnology is. Because the technology is so novel, laboratory results are not good indicators of future manufacturing performance, and doing more process research in the laboratory does not appear to offer lead-time advantages. In many cases, more laboratory research seems to result in longer development lead times. The difference between the development strategies required in biotechnology and those required in chemical-based pharmaceuticals highlights an important lesson: There is no one way to carry out process development that is correct for all situations and technologies; managers must be careful to match their approach to particular constraints and opportunities inherent in the technology itself.

Focus less on organizational structure and more on informal channels of communication. In several of the companies we studied, there was tremendous

Impact of Process Research on Process-Development Lead Times

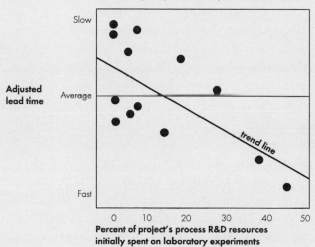

In chemical-based pharmaceuticals, spending more on process research early cuts process-development lead times . . .

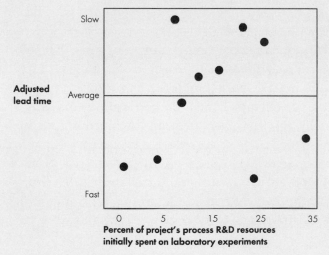

. . . In biotechnology, it does not, which is why no statistically significant trend was detected.

internal debate about how process development should
be organized. Some managers believed that process
development should be part of R&D; others believed
that it should be the responsibility of manufacturing;
and still others believed it was best to have two
groups—one responsible for upstream process research
(part of R&D) and another responsible for downstream
process development, engineering, and scale-up (part of
manufacturing).

Our statistical analyses generated a surprising finding: No single approach provides a consistent advantage.
Having a single integrated group responsible for all
phases of process research and development from the
laboratory to the factory tended to have some advantages in terms of lead times and development costs, but
there were many exceptions. Some integrated groups
were slow and inefficient; others were not. We also
noticed that the organizational home of process R&D
did not seem to matter much. We saw R&D-based
process-development groups with a lot of manufacturing
savvy and manufacturing-based process-development
groups that had much better relationships with R&D
than with the plant.

This lack of consistent findings suggests that informal relationships and approaches to managing projects
tend to matter more than formal structures and procedures. For example, one high-performing company
actually had three organizations involved in process
development: a process-research group (organizationally
and physically collocated with R&D) and two process-
development groups (one in the United States and one
in Europe, each at a manufacturing site). Some projects
passed through all three organizations and sites.

One would think that such multiple transfers would result in excessively long lead times and higher development costs. The company, however, avoided this outcome. There was intensive communication and early-stage problem solving among the people at all three sites. Even more important, scientists at the three sites viewed their roles very broadly and were able to work effectively with personnel at other sites. For example, the chemists at the manufacturing site were not restricted to scaling up the process in the plant. They could and did become involved at a very early stage in the development cycle. Scientists at the other sites held the plant-based scientists in very high regard and routinely called on them to help solve technical problems in their laboratories. Senior managers played a key role in creating a culture that fostered cooperation, communication, integration, and joint problem solving. And their career paths helped explain why they could play such a role. At one point in his career, the head of R&D's process-development group had run process development in a manufacturing organization, and the head of manufacturing's process-development group had once run process development within R&D. Each, then, had a thorough understanding of the challenges that the other faced, and their organizations reflected that understanding.

As the competitive environment has changed in a variety of high-technology industries, many companies have chosen to focus their energies on refining and enhancing their traditional strengths in product research and development and have overlooked the importance of process development. Outstanding high-tech companies that have integrated their product-development skills with a new focus on process development—companies such as Intel in microprocessors and Hewlett-Packard in ink-jet printers—have built a unique and sustainable competitive position without expending more total resources. They have created capabilities that have resulted in faster, more frequent, more productive, and more effective product launches than ever before. They have established a performance standard that those who continue to undervalue process technology are finding increasingly difficult to match.

How Manufacturing Can Make Low-Tech Products High-Tech

LIKE THEIR COUNTERPARTS in high-tech industries, managers in relatively mature industries often fail to see how process-development capabilities can help them differentiate their products. Especially if their companies make consumer products, they look to marketing to differentiate their products and to process development to find ways to lower production costs and improve quality and reliability. Although marketing can help a company create a distinctive image in the marketplace, a company's capability to develop complex, cost-efficient process technologies can help it create distinctive products—even if those products are comparatively low tech. Consider the following two examples.

Gillette Sensor

Introduced in 1990, Gillette's Sensor razor became one of the most successful new products in the history of the razor industry. Unlike existing razor designs with fixed mounted blades, the Sensor incorporated floating blades, which could better follow the contours of a man's face and thus provide a closer shave. Compared with razor designs at the time, the Sensor was a highly complex product, incorporating 23 parts (compared with five pieces for most disposable razors).

Its complexity created stiff manufacturing challenges. For example, because the blades needed to float on springs independently of one another, they had to be much more rigid (to hold their shape) than those in existing systems and therefore had to be mounted on a thick steel bar. Since gluing them to the bar would have been too unreliable, imprecise, and expensive for high-volume manufacturing, Gillette engineers, working with a vendor, developed a laser spot-welder capable of performing 93 highly intricate welds per second—faster than any existing laser. Gillette also needed to develop intricate molds so that it could make the head of the razor (which holds the blades) within tolerances of $\pm.0002$ inches.

Development of the manufacturing processes took more than seven years, required a $75 million investment in R&D, and a $125 million investment in manufacturing equipment. But, in addition to making possible a distinctive product, the manufacturing processes used to make both the razor and its blade have proven to be a major barrier to entry.

Vistakon: Acuvue Disposable Lenses

In June 1988, Johnson & Johnson's Vistakon division introduced Acuvue, the first contact lens designed to be worn continuously and discarded after seven days of wear. Although the concept was novel, the product design was not. The Acuvue was fabricated from the same basic type of polymer used in other soft lenses. And even though the lens was thinner (to permit more oxygen permeability), its basic dimensional design was similar to existing lenses. What was different was the manufacturing technology.

The main attraction of the Acuvue lens was convenience: because the lenses could be disposed of after a short period, they required less cleaning and long-term care than traditional soft lenses (which users keep for about a year). Within three years of Acuvue's introduction, its worldwide sales topped $225 million, catapulting Vistakon into a leading position with about 25% of the U.S. market for contact lenses.

Admittedly, much of the Acuvue's success stems from Johnson & Johnson's ability to identify an unmet need in the marketplace (a convenient contact lens) and its considerable expertise in consumer marketing. However, the company would not have been able to exploit the basic marketing concept had it not developed a new manufacturing process that reduced the cost of the lenses so that consumers could afford literally to throw them away. In addition, they recognized that consumers could not be expected to tolerate minor differences in the corrective power or fit of their lenses from week to week, so they had to manufacture them with an extremely high degree of uniformity.

Vistakon decided that the answer was a manufacturing process that could produce lenses within much tighter tolerances and with signigicantly higher yields than traditional methods could. Tighter tolerances would allow Vistakon to reduce testing and sorting greatly, a process that accounts for about one-third of the cost of manufacturing traditional lenses. The division obtained the process it sought by licensing a radical technology from a Danish company and then refining it over five years. By then, however, competitors were nipping at its heels.

Nevertheless Vistakon was able to ramp up production so rapidly that it could start selling the Acuvue nationally within just a few months after it began commercial manufacturing. Although major competitors introduced their own disposable lenses soon after Vistakon, it took them from six months to a year to ramp up production to the point that they could begin national marketing. Even then, Vistakon's manufacturing costs were significantly lower thanks to its superior process technology. And it has maintained its lead in the disposable market ever since.[6]

Notes

1. Of the 11 companies that participated in our study, 5 were large multinationals, 5 were relatively young biotechnology companies, and one was the biotech division of a major pharmaceutical company. All 23 process-development projects were associated with the launch of a major new drug; 13 involved traditional synthetic-chemical processes and 10 involved biotechnology processes. We used two additional criteria in selecting the projects in our sample: the project had to have been completed (all took place between 1980 and 1994), and the company had to agree to give us access to data on the project's history and performance, as well as the personnel involved. Relying on in-depth interviews with project participants, questionnaires, and proprietary company documents, we collected data on the history and timing of critical project events, resources expended, and the details of approaches

used to identify and solve problems. Given the highly sensitive and proprietary nature of the data we obtained, we agreed with the participating companies to keep their identities confidential. The data-collection process, which occurred between August 1991 and November 1993, involved nearly 200 interviews with personnel from participating research-and-development sites and plants in the United States and Europe. We used statistical analyses to identify systemic factors affecting both lead times and development-productivity performance. See Gary P. Pisano, "Knowledge, Integration, and the Locus of Learning: An Empirical Analysis of Process Development," *Strategic Management Journal*, Volume 15, 1994.

2. Manufacturers of ethical pharmaceuticals received a 132% increase in prices (as measured by the Producer Price Index) during the 1980s compared with the overall inflation rate of 22% for all finished consumer goods. (*Medical and Healthcare Marketplace Guide*, MLR Biomedical Information Services, 9th edition, 1993.)

3. Standard and Poor's Industry Surveys, December 16, 1993.

4. *Pharmaceutical R&D: Costs, Risks, and Rewards*, U.S. Office of Technology Assessment, February 1993.

5. "A Modern Smokestack Industry," *The Economist*, November 14, 1992.

6. "How J&J's Foresight Made Contact Lenses Pay," *Business Week*, May 4, 1992.

Originally published in September–October 1995
Reprint 95506

Real-World R&D

Jumping the Product Generation Gap

MARCO IANSITI

Executive Summary

TRADITIONAL R&D "pipelines" have produced crucial technical innovations, including the transistor. Yet many of today's best high-tech companies have evolved a fundamentally different approach to R&D. Author Marco Iansiti calls this new approach *system focus*. Based on a study of 12 mainframe computer companies that developed a similar product in the 1980s, Iansiti has found that system-focused companies achieve the best product improvements at the lowest cost.

The most striking characteristic of system focus in the formation of an *integration team*. A good integration team adapts new technologies to what a company already knows how to do. Moreover, it enhances current systems to take advantage of those new ideas. Integration team members work on a stream of related projects, forming a cohesive unit that develops from project to project. And such continuity over product generations can save a company hundreds of millions of dollars— effectively jumping the usual generation gap in traditional R&D organizations, where knowledge is often lost or unintegrated over time.

In a case-history comparison of "Traditional Company A" and "System-Focused Company B," Iansiti demonstrates how this can happen. In Company A, researchers hand off a completed technical concept to development engineers without actively investigating the challenge of high-volume production first. But by stressing the entire system rather than focusing narrowly on individual tasks, or artificially separating the research stage from development, Company B avoids recurring production problems and a design that's incompatible with the existing manufacturing system.

In most companies, the R&D process follows a well-trodden, familiar path. First comes basic research, in which the scientists in charge explore a new concept— say, a new polymer. Next, scientists with specific knowledge of the research area improve the concept until they identify an application for the polymer, such as a new insulating material. Finally, they hand off the job of actually developing a commercial product and its manufacturing process to engineers down the line.

I think of this traditional R&D approach as a series of successive refinements, one group of experts after another adding its contribution to the developing product. Such a linear approach tends to compartmentalize specific knowledge; a particular part of the R&D process may even be restricted to a single researcher.

Certainly the traditional R&D pipeline, based on the assumption that the greatest challenge to developing new products lies in making scientific discoveries, has led to significant innovations, such as the transistor and the color television. Yet I will argue that many of the best high-tech companies, particularly in the computer industry, have evolved a fundamentally different approach to new product development, one that is much more efficient and better suited to today's R&D complexities.

This new approach, which I call *system focus*, integrates the entire R&D process, rather than just shooting projects down a narrow pipeline. Based on a study of the R&D organizations of 12 mainframe computer companies—AT&T, Bull, DEC, Fujitsu, Hitachi, IBM, ICL, Mitsubishi Electric, NEC, Siemens, Toshiba, and Unisys— my research associates and I have determined that system-focused companies achieve the best product improvements in the shortest time and at the lowest cost. This is no small feat in the high-tech industry, where rolling out new, technically challenging products at the right time has been the key to success for more than a decade.

We compared the approaches these R&D organizations took during the 1980s in developing new technology for a particular product: the multichip module. Mainframe multichip modules house and connect the computer's most crucial integrated circuits, affecting the entire system's speed and reliability. They thus present an extremely complex and technically challenging development task, precisely the type of R&D hurdle most companies now face, whether they produce computers, cars, or pharmaceuticals.

The different approaches these companies took toward the multichip module demonstrate how a product, its manufacturing process, and the needs of its users constitute a system and should be developed as such. Any change in this product system—for example, the use of a more reliable material in the production of the module's substrate—will change the entire design and manufacturing process. In turn, these changes can lead to development dead ends, longer product rollouts, and many wasted hours if not accounted for from the very beginning. Therefore, the goal of new product development shifts from simply incorporating a powerful new element to optimizing the whole system.

High-tech companies are most affected by volatile markets and the rapid pace of technological change. But while industries that have traditionally been considered science-based, such as aerospace and semiconductors, may feel the most pressure to adapt their R&D approach, the challenge of incorporating new technical developments into commercial products is now a reality of competition in many other industries as well. From the application of laser-welding in the Lexus LS 400 automobile to the use of composite materials in the construction industry, new technical concepts have fueled innovations in a wide range of products. Improving the speed and efficiency of product development has, indeed, become a major competitive weapon.

The Integration Team

When it comes to R&D resources, principally the time and people involved, the most striking characteristic of a system-focused approach is the central role of *technology integration*. By this I mean the integration of the R&D process within a company, not the "fusion" of different technologies to create new products, although technology fusion often does result in complex components like the multichip module.

System-focused companies form a core group of managers, scientists, and engineers at the earliest stages of the R&D process. This *integration team* investigates the impact of various technical choices on the design of the product and the manufacturing system. The team's main objective is to balance

A good integration team adapts new technologies to what a company already knows how to do.

new research from the lab with the manufacturing system's existing capabilities. A good integration team adapts new technologies to what a company already knows how to do. And more than that, it enhances the current system to take advantage of those new ideas.

In fact, all of the system-focused companies in our study established integration teams in the early stages to handle technology integration for the multichip module. Some of the companies went so far as to build pilot plants in order to experiment with new technologies, a sizable but worthwhile investment since it often provided unambiguous information on future production yields and manufacturing costs.

What follows is a typical profile for a successful integration team. In general, the members are the foundation of a system-focused approach to R&D. They possess a T-shaped combination of skills: they are not only experts in specific technical areas but also intimately acquainted with the potential systemic impact of their particular tasks. On the one hand, they have a deep knowledge of a discipline like ceramic materials engineering, represented by the vertical stroke of the T.

On the other hand, these ceramic specialists also know how their discipline interacts with others, such as polymer processing—the T's horizontal top stroke.

Note that in the system-focused companies we studied, the fact that team members had this combination of skills was no accident. Team leaders considered their most important job to be assigning projects that would develop individuals by providing learning opportunities in other areas. According to one of the project managers we interviewed, "Each engineer is responsible for lots of different parts of the project. We choose the pieces to stretch their knowledge."

Successful integration teams specify and design both the product and the manufacturing process, leading the way in choosing new equipment. The team works with both system and component designers (for example, both mainframe designers and chip developers), facilitating a clearer understanding of how individual product components will interact. In fact, the integration team is usually in daily contact with the manufacturing plant. Team members often deal with major production problems on ongoing product lines, which allows them to evaluate the impact of new technology on production. And as a development project progresses, the team physically moves to the site of major technical difficulties, such as the pilot or manufacturing facility.

For projects that jump several product generations, system focus can end up saving hundreds of millions of dollars.

Perhaps most important of all, the integration team works on a stream of related products, forming a cohesive unit of engineers who develop from project to project. Retained over multiple product generations, team members become the company's repository of technically integrated "system" knowledge. While various research groups continue to develop and present new options, it is the integration team that turns new ideas into useful work by conceptualizing new products and providing continuity.

Such continuity over product generations pays off. Even when it comes to individual research projects, system-focused companies can save many years of staff effort and development time. (See the graph "Finding the R&D 'Sweet Spot.'") Even one less engineer working on a project saves roughly $100,000 a year; for projects like the multichip module, which extend over a decade and across product generations, the difference between traditional R&D and system focus can amount to hundreds of millions of dollars.

Of course, an emphasis on technology integration should not cut into the status of a company's research

Finding the R&D "Sweet Spot"

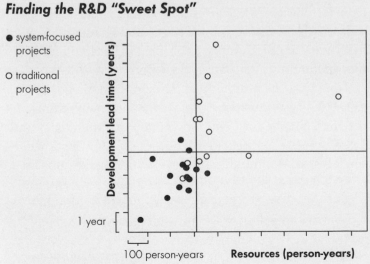

Note: *This data was adjusted for differences in the technical complexity of individual projects.*

organization. I believe that for system focus to succeed, basic researchers must provide the integration team with a broad array of technical possibilities. Most integration teams will have a natural bias toward using older approaches to materials and manufacturing, because that's what team members are familiar with. However, research (whether conducted internally or by outside suppliers) must offset this potential inertia by championing a variety of alternatives. Though they frequently used suppliers to provide additional technical options, the most successful companies in our study had vibrant internal research organizations of their own.

Research: System Focus versus the Traditional Pipeline

When the traditional research pipeline and system focus are examined side by side, their differences are clear. Let's start by comparing them during the research phase, when scientist-engineers investigate new technical possibilities for upcoming product generations. The following case histories of "Traditional Company A" and "System-Focused Company B," loosely based on companies in our study, illustrate the differences.

Note that the multichip module provides a good example of *development complexity* and its inherent research challenges. (See "Development Complexity and System Focus" at the end of this article.) For instance, the latest IBM multichip module, which makes up the core of its new ES9000 mainframe computer, contains more than 65 stacked layers of electrical circuits that total about one mile of wiring—all packed on a five-inch-square flat piece of ceramic.

In such complex projects, the research phase involves more than coming up with a new material or production technique. It also includes technology integration in the form of a *technical concept*: a detailed specification of how the complete set of technical options will combine to provide the new product with good quality and low cost. While the research group controls technology integration in traditional companies, in a system-focused company the integration team takes charge.

TRADITIONAL COMPANY A

The research group at Company A explored a new ceramic material composition that could conduct a lot of heat. Using scaled-down equipment in the lab, these researchers fabricated small quantities of the material. They surveyed the literature, communicated intensively with scientists at universities, and performed many small-scale experiments aimed at characterizing the new material's properties, including its detailed microstructure. All of their research led them to believe that this new ceramic material could increase the speed and reliability of their company's multichip module.

Obviously, these researchers had much to gain if their ceramic was adopted, and they aggressively championed this material. They subsequently won: senior managers allowed them to develop their concept for the entire module system. Therefore, the same scientists who had launched the initial investigations were then responsible for integrating their new materials into a functional system.

Yet their sole criterion for success was feasibility: they had only to fabricate a small number of prototypes using lab equipment. The group eventually produced several partially functional modules, which showed that it ought to be possible to build a real module based on the new ceramic.

Once the technical concept had proved feasible, technology integration, driven by the research group, was complete. The basic technologies and the product design were set—which is fine, if both hold up in the real world of manufacturing. But in this case, the technical concept became a foregone conclusion without an active investigation of the challenge of future high-volume production. In fact, the activities of the research group ended at this point, and the module project was deemed ready for development.

SYSTEM-FOCUSED COMPANY B

Here an integration team, formed at the very beginning of the R&D process, led the multichip module project. These 20 scientists and engineers monitored the basic investigations conducted by the research group as well as those contracted to several outside ceramic materials suppliers. As the results from initial research came in, the integration team began selecting the most promising of the various new techniques and worked on combining the elements into one technical concept. They investigated several possible technical concepts in parallel, based on different combinations of materials, such as aluminum and glass ceramic substrates.

This stage took much more time and involved more resources than the explorations of Company A. (See the chart "From Concept to Product: Slimming Down Development.") As the integration team learned more about the systemic effects of the various alternatives, some were dropped, others postponed for future generations, and others refined and kept for further study. Of course, this weeding of alternatives contrasted sharply with the process at Company A, where the initial research group championed their ceramic material and focused on demonstrating its feasibility.

In fact, Company B's integration team did not identify feasibility as an explicit requirement for their technical alternatives. They gradually selected the most promising concepts, using a steady, ongoing selection process designed to solve problems largely ignored by Company A's researchers: manufacturability, yield, and reliability.

And as the integration process steadily continued, other groups became more involved. Equipment suppliers, for example, worked directly with integration team

From Concept to Product: Slimming Down Development

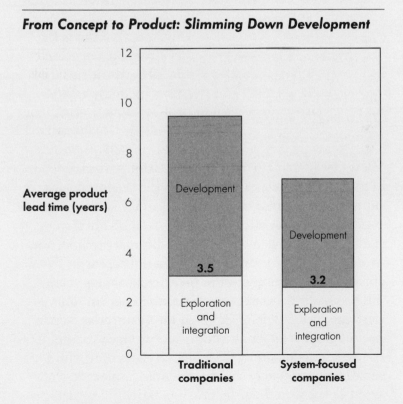

members to specify the production tooling for the new system. Engineers from various development groups and the manufacturing facility discussed the details of the production process. It was only at this point that the integration team finally committed to a single new concept and froze the basic design of their company's multichip module.

COMPETING PHILOSOPHIES

Clearly, Company A and Company B represent fundamentally different approaches to the exploration and selection of new technology. Under the traditional R&D philosophy of companies like A, researchers assume that discovering new scientific possibilities is the critical challenge and involves the identification and early exploration of new ideas. While the traditional R&D pipeline certainly

One frustrated development engineer said: "By the time we got involved, the basic technologies were more than 90% established."

allows for freedom in early investigations, its main aim is to select a concept that includes the technical possibilities with the maximum *theoretical* impact on future product characteristics, as proven "feasible" in the lab.

The critical weakness of the traditional method, however, is that it does not characterize the *actual* impact of the technical concept on the product and manufacturing process before selecting a winning concept. This is particularly a problem when a given research project is part of a much larger and complex "product system" like the multichip module. The research group first optimizes the technology chosen, and the development group is left with the problem of making the system work. As one frustrated development engineer put it, "By the time we got involved, the basic technologies were more than 90% established."

In contrast, the system-focused philosophy emphasizes discovering and capturing knowledge about the interactions between new research in the lab and the company's existing product and manufacturing systems. At Company B, the goal was joint optimization of system and technology, even though that initially consumed more time and resources. An integration team encouraged unbiased investigation of many alternatives, but its selection was greatly influenced by the details of the existing system. One engineer at a system-focused company in our study said, "The most essential part of choosing a new technology is to establish its impact on the production process. And we still never get it quite right."

That in no way means that system-focused companies like B settle for less aggressive results. In our study, we repeatedly observed that traditional companies like A often developed individual elements that were superior to B's—for example, ceramic materials with better electrical and thermal properties. Yet system-focused companies still achieved superior overall performance because technology integration from the start of the R&D project more than compensated for apparently inferior materials. In other words, the traditional R&D pipeline adds up to a whole that is less than the sum of its parts, while system focus produces a whole greater than the sum of its parts.

Development: How System-Focused Companies Get Results

Although comparing the research phases in Company A and Company B shows the importance of system focus, it's in the development of new products that the approaches yield dramatically different results. The "Multichip Module Project Maps" provide graphic evidence of why system-focused companies ultimately save on both time and money in rolling out new products and their subsequent generations.

COMPANY A

When it came time for Traditional Company A to implement the new ceramic material for the multichip module, the resources devoted to the project mushroomed. As you can see in the project map for Company A, a large development group was necessary because of the difficulty of increasing production yields and product reliability. Many of the details of the winning technical concept turned out to be extremely difficult for Company A to implement.

As the head of development for a traditional company in our study observed, "We completely underestimated what it would be like to ramp up." After extensively redesigning the product and manufacturing process, the development group transferred the new multichip module system to the production facility. But pilot production also proved difficult, requiring additional design changes. After many false starts, targeted yields were finally achieved, volume production began, and the development group moved on to the next generation of module, taking over their end once more from the research group.

Due to promotions and individual career choices, many of these development engineers shifted to unrelated projects. In all, it took Company A over $6^{1}/_{2}$ years of development time and about 800 person-years of

Multichip Module Project Maps

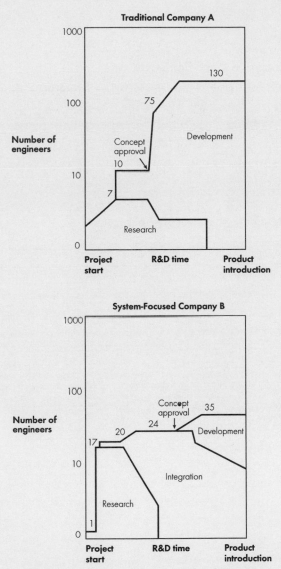

For most companies, a project really begins in earnest at the concept approval stage. The introductory research phase is considered quite cheap compared to the resources allocated for development.

engineering and scientific activity to complete the development phase.

COMPANY B

In contrast, System-Focused Company B completed the development phase in less than $4^{1}/_{2}$ years and 300 person-years. The chart "How Many Engineers Does It Take?" indicates the big difference in average resources used during development. In Company B, the integration team, which had been responsible for the basic

---

How Many Engineers Does It Take?

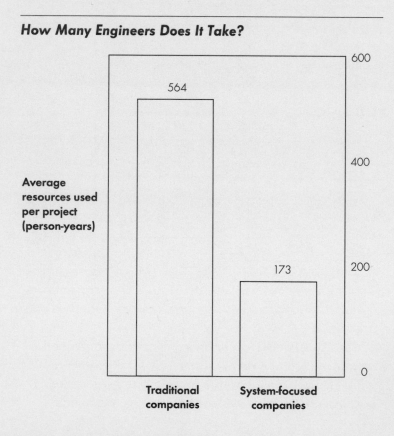

Average resources used per project (person-years)

564 — Traditional companies

173 — System-focused companies

600
400
200
0

conceptual design, remained in charge of the project
during development. A few team members worked part-
time on integration of the next generation. Most were
deeply involved with development, working directly at
the plant or with materials suppliers.

As development progressed, integration team members gradually shifted to work on the next generation;
yet the team still led the process until the plant had
achieved full production yields. Many members continued to be responsible for production yields even after
the product had been introduced, and they were called
into the plant when major problems occurred. In fact,
the same people who were responsible for improving
production yields of the current generation also often
worked on specifying the technical concept for the next
generation.

ORGANIZATIONAL LEARNING

System-focused companies like Company B capture
knowledge about the different elements of the entire
R&D process and feed that knowledge back in at the
technology integration stage. At Company B, involving
engineers in the integration of several product generations allowed them to transfer valuable knowledge all
along the line. This *upstream* transfer of information
provides not only continuity from generation to generation but also continual learning about the impact of new
technology on the complex production capabilities of an
organization.

And this transfer of knowledge goes beyond good
communication. Organizational learning promotes individual learning, especially for integration team members. As one team leader noted, "At this point, one

person is product engineer and production engineer at the same time. Basically, we no longer have the luxury of spending a lot of time communicating." The example "A System-Focused Résumé" illustrates how an engineer gains integration knowledge over several product generations.

A System-Focused Résumé

The hypothetical "Mr. Furube," a typical engineer at a system-focused mainframe computer company, is 30 years old. In less than a decade, he has worked on three generations of the same product.

Mr. Furube

1991–1992	Engineer Currently designing chip set for gen 3 mainframe.
1989–1990	Massachusetts Institute of Technology: M.S. in Electrical Engineering.
1987–1989	Worker and Trainer Developed gen 2 module assembly process, working with suppliers. Designed, ordered, and set up production machines for microchip carrier.
1985–1986	Worker Improved production process for gen 1.5 module. Conducted feasibility study for new gen 2 module concept. Worked on basic conceptual design of gen 2 module; applied for patent.
1983–1984	Trainee Developed production process for LSI modules for gen 1 mainframe; set up specialized machines and trained workers on pilot production line. Designed production process for gen 1.5 module.
1979–1983	Tokyo University, degree in mechanical engineering.

Traditional companies like Company A devote substantial attention to the transfer of knowledge but only *downstream*—through the narrow pipeline of research to development to manufacturing. Under this approach, there is no mechanism for transferring knowledge back upstream so that it can improve the next round of technology selection and integration. Moreover, the compartmentalized knowledge typical of traditional R&D pipelines often disappears as scientists, engineers, and product developers shift from one project to another or take other jobs.

Given this distinction in organizational learning, it's not surprising that the system-focused companies in our study were faster and more productive on individual projects *and* that the performance gap between traditional companies and system-focused ones actually increased over time. We found a substantial difference between resources used in subsequent product generations for traditional and system-focused companies. The resources used by the system-focused companies each decreased dramatically as integration teams learned more and more about the product and its manufacturing system. When it comes to jumping the product generation gap, efficiently transferring knowledge is essential.

In contrast, companies that relied on the traditional R&D pipeline decreased in productivity over successive product generations. Competitive pressures to keep up with increasing technological innovations led them to increase the resources they sunk into technology development. Yet without fundamental changes to the whole R&D process—namely, the use of integration teams to facilitate organizational learning—their R&D became even less efficient than before.

Integrated Problem Solving

The companies I've been calling system-focused depart from the traditional R&D pipeline both in philosophy and organizational design. They also differ significantly in their approach to solving problems. Our study included 61 different problem-solving attempts. While the traditional companies took a relatively narrow approach to solving problems, the system-focused companies were remarkable for the breadth of theirs. Consider the following example.

PROBLEM

The core of this multichip module contains more than 40 ceramic layers, each one carrying a complex circuit. The layers first are patterned, then stacked, and finally fired together at a high temperature. However, as the ceramic bakes, it shrinks. Therefore, the challenge is to achieve uniform shrinkage without buckling so that the module retains its shape and has a smooth surface for connecting integrated circuits.

SOLUTION A

Scientists at Company A identified the buckling problem early on in the research phase. At this point, they worked with a simplified model of the multichip module core, using scaled-down equipment in the lab. After making a number of adjustments to the ceramic composition and the firing process, they succeeded in eliminating the buckling.

Later, during the development phase, a more representative model of the multichip module was used on a new pilot production line, which closely—though not exactly—represented the manufacturing conditions of volume production. The buckling problem reoccurred. Development engineers spent much time and energy adjusting the ceramic material and the production process in order to fix the problem again.

At the end of the development phase, the new product was moved to the actual manufacturing plant. Once again, the buckling reoccurred, causing additional delays in the production schedule. After a great deal of effort, the third and final round of reengineering succeeded in eliminating the problem for good.

SOLUTION B

For scientists at Company B, the problem wasn't narrowly defined as "how to eliminate all buckling" but instead as "how to get the entire system to function effectively." The integration team focused earlier on a prototype of the product and the manufacturing process, using a pilot production line with equipment representative of actual conditions but flexible enough to allow experimentation.

Developing a module prototype that was representative of high-volume production conditions allowed the team at Company B to characterize precisely the extent of the buckling. And by asking a broader question at the start and drawing on a broader knowledge base, the integration team found a faster and cheaper solution: controlling the buckling and coating the ceramic substrate with a polymer to smooth the surface. When the project moved from research into development, the buckling problem did not reoccur.

In fact, the system-focused companies in our study were only slightly better at identifying problems early on; they identified 74% of the significant problems in multichip module development, but the more traditional companies found 61% of their own early problems. The most striking difference came in achieving real rather than apparent solutions. Only 40% of the early fixes made by traditional companies stood up to the requirements of later project phases. Yet 77% of the early solutions discovered by system-focused companies actually worked in the long run.

A New R&D Philosophy

System focus is a philosophy rather than a specific technique, one that underpins and reinforces the importance of technology integration: the mutual adaptation of new technology, product design, manufacturing process, and user needs. An engineer from a system-focused company said, "We get together with the semiconductor and systems group people to discuss future possibilities. Everyone talks about this, and negotiations occur throughout. There's lots of give-and-take."

Compare this remark with that of an R&D manager from a traditional company: "The strategy is always to take a piece of the technology and set up a group to own it. If coordination problems exist, we set up a task force." These two remarks reveal fundamentally different assumptions about what R&D is all about.

Most companies that live by a system-focused philosophy emphasize the work of an integration team during all phases of a project. Yet the substantial advantages of technology integration don't come without investment and the commitment of senior managers as well. It takes time to develop the skills of integration teams. The new approach may appear slow and cumbersome at first.

And even after good results start to roll in, team leaders and senior managers still may need periodically to redirect the work of individual team members, helping them to fight inertia.

Still, the most effective companies in our study demonstrated the value of system focus in an environment that is both complex and changeable. Their experience shows that an integration team can build a solid and powerful base of knowledge about the interactions between the most critical decisions in the design of a new product. Of course, while similar in purpose and character, integration teams of various organizations will develop different focuses depending on the nature of the technical environment. In high-performance computer processor design, the link between material choice and manufacturability presents the toughest challenge. Therefore, successful integration teams, like those responsible for the multichip module projects in our study, will emphasize retaining detailed knowledge of the impact past materials choices have had on manufacturing.

In contrast, the pharmaceutical industry provides a very different set of R&D challenges. Integration teams there would find that the most complex interactions are between the chemical formulation of a new drug and its safety and efficacy, as perceived by both users and regulatory agencies. In this case, these would replace manufacturing difficulties and history as the foundation of a rich R&D knowledge base.

But regardless of the industry, the traditional R&D pipeline is not up to managing technology integration in any environment that is characterized by development complexity. A company marketing cosmetics, for example, had to postpone rolling out a new product because

its novel chemical formulation proved incompatible
with the planned packaging. A forest products company
barely avoided the complete failure of a new venture in
engineered wood products; it discovered in the nick of
time that there were subtle inconsistencies between the
preset production process (which had been optimized
for northern pine) and the properties of southern
pine.

And a pharmaceutical company failed to obtain
approval for a new cancer drug due to poor integration
of regulatory requirements and the development process. A competitor with a more system-focused
approach integrated its regulatory activities and drug
formulation accordingly and was able to roll out the new
drug, gaining sole access to a very large market.

With sophisticated customers who demand greater
performance and new, aggressive, and often subtle product characteristics, developing successful products
requires managing an increasing number of complex
design decisions. Compared with old-line industries,
which carefully nurtured deep knowledge of narrow
specifics, today's shifting markets call for a flexible
breadth of experience, backed by the organizational and
technical ability to integrate.

For system focus to work, then, the company must
have a consistent technology strategy and view the
whole R&D process as a continuous stream of compe-
tence-building projects, not as a series of isolated efforts.
Successful companies will target core technical areas
and gradually build technology integration in those
areas. Such a consistent approach, driven by the long-
term commitment of senior managers, will allow integration teams to acquire the knowledge, tools, and procedures necessary for the efficient integration of new

technology, ultimately producing the innovative products that customers want.

Development Complexity and System Focus

WHEN THE ENTIRE R&D process becomes system-
focused, companies are in a much better position to wres-
tle with the development complexity inherent in the creation of today's new products. Development complexity
refers to the complications of the R&D process itself, not
what the end product looks like or how difficult it is to
manufacture.

For example, the development of drugs involves integrating many different research decisions based on
knowledge of pharmacology, toxicology, physiology, relevant body systems, regulatory requirements in dozens of
countries, and differences in medical practice and custom
in those countries. But ironically enough, the pill that
results from such a complicated set of R&D decisions is
often so simple it can be manufactured in a home laboratory. This illustrates how bringing successful drugs quickly
to market depends much more on integrating the knowledge of all R&D factors at every point in the process than
on pure scientific prowess.

Of course, the development complexity that characterizes an industry can change over time, often in response
to competitive pressures for products that deliver higher
performance. Twenty years ago, automobiles were
assembled from discrete and largely independent parts.
But today's cars can be more accurately described as
integrated systems rather than assembled parts. Conse-

quently, a tight fit between individual design decisions is essential to satisfying customer expectations.

Now automobile manufacturers frequently "tune" the noise characteristics of a car to match the expectations of the market it is designed to serve. That means a high-revving sports car has a much different sound quality—as well as overall ride—than a luxury car. Such specific R&D challenges require a focus on the entire system, since decisions in basic engine design must be linked to the structural properties of the chassis, right down to the acoustical properties of the felt used in floor mats.

Originally published in May–June 1993
Reprint 93307

How Architecture Wins Technology Wars

CHARLES R. MORRIS AND

CHARLES H. FERGUSON

Executive Summary

SIGNS OF REVOLUTIONARY TRANSFORMATION in the global computer industry are everywhere. A roll call of the major industry players reads like a waiting list in the emergency room.

The usual explanations for the industry's turmoil are at best inadequate. Scale, friendly government policies, manufacturing capabilities, a strong position in desktop markets, excellent software, top design skills—none of these is sufficient, either by itself or in combination, to ensure competitive success in information technology.

A new paradigm is required to explain patterns of success and failure. Simply stated, success flows to the company that manages to establish proprietary architectural control over a broad, fast-moving, competitive space.

Architectural strategies have become crucial to information technology because of the astonishing rate of improvement in microprocessors and other semiconductor components. Since no single vendor can keep pace with the outpouring of cheap, powerful, mass-produced components, customers insist on stitching together their own local systems solutions. Architectures impose order on the system and make the interconnections possible. The architectural controller is the company that controls the standard by which the entire information package is assembled. Microsoft's Windows is an excellent example of this. Because of the popularity of Windows, companies like Lotus must conform their software to its parameters in order to compete for market share.

In the 1990s, proprietary architectural control is not only possible but indispensable to competitive success. What's more, it has broader implications for organizational structure: architectural competition is giving rise to a new form of business organization.

THE GLOBAL COMPUTER INDUSTRY is undergoing radical transformation. IBM, the industry's flagship, is reeling from unaccustomed losses and is reducing staff by the tens of thousands. The very survival of DEC, the industry's number two company, is open to question. A roll call of the larger computer companies—Data General, Unisys, Bull, Olivetti, Siemens, Prime—reads like a waiting list in the emergency room.

What's more, the usual explanations for the industry's turmoil are at best inadequate. It is true, for example, that centralized computing is being replaced by desktop technology. But how to explain the recent troubles at Compaq, the desktop standard setter through much of the 1980s? Or the battering suffered by IBM's PC business and most of the rest of the desktop clone makers, Asian and Western alike?

And the Japanese, for once, are unconvincing as a culprit. The fear that Japanese manufacturing prowess would sweep away the Western computer industry has not materialized. True, Japanese companies dominate many commodity markets, but they have been losing share, even in products they were expected to control, like laptop computers. Earnings at their leading electronics and computer companies have been as inglorious as those of Western companies.

Explanations that look to the continuing shift in value added from hardware to software, while containing an important truth, are still too limited. Lotus has one of the largest installed customer bases in the industry. Nevertheless, the company has been suffering through some very rough times. Meanwhile, Borland continues to pile up losses.

Nor are innovation and design skills a surefire recipe for success. LSI Logic and Cypress Semiconductor are among the most innovative and well-managed companies in the industry, yet they still lose money. Design-based "fabless," "computerless" companies such as MIPS have fared very badly too. MIPS was saved from bankruptcy only by a friendly takeover. And Chips and Technologies is in dire straits.

Government protection and subsidies are no panacea either. The European computer industry is the most heavily subsidized in the world but still has no serious players in global computer markets.

Scale, friendly government policies, world-class manufacturing prowess, a strong position in desktop markets, excellent software, top design and innovative skills—none of these, it seems, is sufficient, either by itself or in combination with each other, to ensure competitive success in this field.

A new paradigm is required to explain patterns of competitive success and failure in information technology. Simply stated, competitive success flows to the company that manages to establish proprietary architectural control over a broad, fast-moving, competitive space.

Architectural strategies have become of paramount importance in information technology because of the astonishing rate of improvement in microprocessors and other semiconductor components. The performance/price ratio of cheap processors is roughly doubling every eighteen months or so, sweeping greater and greater expanses of the information industry within the reach of ever-smaller and less expensive machines. Since no single vendor can keep pace with the deluge of cheap, powerful, mass-produced components, customers insist on stitching together their own local system solutions. Architectures impose order on the system and make the interconnections possible.

> *Proprietary architectures are not only possible but also indispensable to competitive success.*

An architectural controller is a company that controls one or more of the standards by which the entire information package is assembled. Much current conventional wisdom argues that, in an "open-systems" era, proprietary architectural control is no longer possible, or even desirable. In fact, the exact opposite is true. In an open-systems era, architectural coherence becomes even more necessary. While any single product is apt to become quickly outdated, a well-designed and open-ended architecture can evolve along with critical technologies, providing a fixed point of stability for customers and serving as the platform for a radiating and long-lived product family.

Proprietary architectures in open systems are not only possible but also indispensable to competitive success—and are also in the best interest of the consumer. They will become increasingly critical as the worlds of computers, telecommunication, and consumer electronics continue to converge.

Architectures in Open Systems

In order to understand architecture as a tool for competitive success in information technology, consider first the many components that make up a typical information system and the types of companies that supply those components.

Take the computer configuration in a typical Wall Street trading or brokerage operation. Powerful workstations with 50 MIPS (millions of instructions per second)—comparable to the power of standard mainframes—sit on every desk. The workstations are connected in a network so they can communicate with each other or with several others at a time. Teams of workstations can be harnessed together to crunch away on a truly big problem. Powerful computers called servers support the network and manage the huge databases—bond pricing histories, for instance—from which the workstations draw.

Such a modern network will be almost entirely open, or externally accessible by other vendors; critical elements, from perhaps as many as a hundred vendors, plug interchangeably into the network. The workstations themselves are from companies like Sun Microsystems, Hewlett-Packard, and IBM, or they may be powerful personal computers from Apple or any of a number of IBM-compatible PC manufacturers. IBM and Hewlett-Packard make their own workstation microprocessors; most workstation or personal computer makers buy microprocessors from companies like Intel, Motorola, Texas Instruments, LSI Logic, AMD, and Cyrix. Almost all the display screens are made in Japan by Sony, NEC, and many other companies; the disk drives come from American companies like Seagate or Conner Peripherals. The memory chips are made in Japan or Korea. The network printers will typically have laser printing engines from Japan or, if they are high-performance printers, from Xerox or IBM; the powerful processors needed to control modern printers will come from AMD, Motorola, or Intel. The rest of the standardized hardware components on the network, like modems, accelerator boards, coprocessors, network interface boards, and the like, will be made by a wide variety of Asian and American companies.

The network will have many layers of software, most of it "shrink-wrapped" from American companies. The operating system—the software that controls the basic interaction of a computer's components—may be a version of AT&T's UNIX, specially tailored by the workstation vendor, as with Sun and IBM, or it may come from a third party, like Microsoft. Many vendors, like Lotus and Borland,

A small handful of innovative companies will define and control a network's critical architectures.

will supply applications software. The complex software required to manage the interaction of the servers and workstations on the network will, in most cases, be supplied by Novell. The software that converts digital data into instructions for printer engines is sold by Hewlett-Packard, Adobe, or one of their many clones. Each smaller element in the system, like a modem or video accelerator, will have its own specialized software, often supplied by a vendor other than the manufacturer.

It is possible to construct open systems of this kind because for each layer of the network there are published standards and interface protocols that allow hardware and software products from many vendors to blend seamlessly into the network. The standards define how programs and commands will work and how data will move around the system—the communication protocols and formats that hardware components must adhere to, the rules for exchanging signals between applications software and the operating system, the processor's command structure, the allowable font descriptions for a printer, and so forth. We call this complex of standards and rules an "architecture."

A small handful of the companies supplying components to the network will define and control the system's critical architectures, each for a specific layer of the system. The architectural standard setters typically include the microprocessor designer (such as Sun or Intel); operating system vendors (possibly Sun or Microsoft); the network system (usually Novell); the printer page-description system (Adobe or Hewlett-Packard); and a small number of others, depending on the nature of the network. Each of these is a proprietary architecture; although the rules for transmitting signals to an Intel processor, for example, are published openly for all vendors, the underlying design of the processor is owned by Intel, just as the design of Sun's operating system is owned by Sun, and so on for Microsoft's Windows/DOS, Novell's Netware, or Adobe's PostScript.

Companies that control proprietary architectural standards have an advantage over other vendors. Since they control the architecture, they are usually better positioned to develop products that maximize its capabilities; by modifying the architecture, they can discipline competing product vendors. In an open-systems era, the most consistently successful information technology companies will be the ones who manage to establish a proprietary architectural standard over a substantial competitive space and defend it against the assaults of both clones and rival architectural sponsors.

It has been conventional wisdom to argue that users, and the cause of technological progress, are better served by *nonproprietary* systems architectures. This is emphatically untrue. There are many examples of nonproprietary architectures, like the CCITT fax standard or the NTSC television standard, most of them established by government bodies or industry groups. Because they are set by committees, they usually settle on lowest-common-denominator, compromise solutions. And they are hard to change. The NTSC has been upgraded only once (for color) in a half-century; committees have been squabbling over an improved fax standard for years. *Proprietary* architectures, by contrast, because they are such extremely valuable franchises, are under constant competitive attack and must be vigorously defended. It is this dynamic that compels a very rapid pace of technological improvement.

Architectural Competitions

The computer industry has been competing on architecture for years. Take the example of the product that established IBM's dominance in the mainframe computer business—the IBM System/360. The 360 was arguably the first pervasive, partially open, information technology architecture. In the late 1960s, once the System/360 became the dominant mainframe solution, IBM began to unbundle component pricing and selectively open the

For over 20 years in the mainframe business, IBM has played this game brilliantly and won every time.

system, in part because of government pressure. Published standards permitted competitors and component suppliers to produce a wide range of IBM-compatible products and programs that were interchangeable with, and sometimes superior to, IBM's own. By licensing its MVS operating system to Amdahl, for example, IBM made it possible for Fujitsu, Amdahl's partner, to produce clones of the IBM mainframe. Much of what was not licensed away voluntarily was acquired anyway by the Japanese through massive intellectual property theft.

Hundreds of new companies selling IBM-compatible mainframe products and software placed intense competitive pressure on IBM. But they also assured that the IBM standard would always be pervasive throughout the mainframe computing world. As a result, even today IBM controls some two-thirds of the IBM-compatible mainframe market and an even higher share of its profits, not only for central processing units but also for disk drives, systems software, and aftermarket products like expanded memory. Because they have no choice but to maintain compatibility with the IBM standard, competitors must wait to reverse-engineer IBM products after they are introduced. Typically, by the time competitive products are on the market, IBM is well down the learning curve or already moving on to the next generation. And as the owner of the dominant architecture, IBM can subtly and precisely raise the hurdles whenever a particular competitor begins to pose a threat. For over 20 years, in generation after generation, IBM has played this game brilliantly and won every time.

Ironically, IBM badly fumbled an equivalent opportunity in desktop computing, handing over the two most critical PC architectural control points—the systems software and the microprocessor—to Microsoft and Intel. Since any clone maker could acquire the operating system software from Microsoft and the microprocessor from Intel, making PCs became a brutal commodity business. As a high-cost manufacturer, IBM now holds only about 15% of the market it created.

In a related error, Compaq made the mistake of assuming that IBM would always control the PC architectural standard. On that premise, the company geared its cost structure and pricing policy to IBM's, only to find itself almost fatally vulnerable when the savage PC price wars of the early 1990s exposed the commoditized character of PC manufacturing. Tellingly, while IBM and Compaq struggle to eke out profits from their PC businesses, Microsoft and Intel are enjoying after-tax margins of about 20%, on sales of more than $4 billion and $6 billion respectively, and together they have more cash than IBM.

For a similar example, consider the case of Lotus. Lotus got its start in a market—spreadsheet software—

where products are complex and feature-rich, hardly commodities. And over the years, the company acquired or developed a broad array of other products—Jazz, Manuscript, Improv, AmiPro, Notes, and Freelance—some of which are technically excellent. Lotus's competitive problem, however, is that these products lack any deep architectural commonality. Indeed, even the embedded spreadsheet software in the company's various offerings is incompatible from one to another.

Point product vendors like Lotus can be very profitable for a time. However, they are always at risk when an architectural leader changes the rules of the game. For example, while Lotus was accumulating a grab bag of point products, Microsoft was creating an architectural lock on the graphical user interface (GUI) for DOS-based computers. (See "Scenarios for Architectural Competition: Graphical User Interfaces" at the end of this article.) And Windows now defines the environment in which Lotus's software must compete. The great power of Windows is that it creates a relatively simple, intuitive, and reasonably uniform interface between a user and a very wide range of applications software. As users become accustomed to the greater ease of Windows, they insist on it, and point product vendors like Lotus are forced to adapt their software to run under the Windows architecture. But Microsoft also offers its own line of point products, like Excel and Word, and since they arguably better exploit the Windows architecture, they are steadily encroaching on Lotus's market share.

The irony is that for a time in the 1980s, Lotus had such a powerful market position that it almost certainly could have established a GUI standard itself. But the company neglected to do so. Such strategic errors spell the difference between an architectural winner and loser.

Principles and Phases of Architectural Competition

There are five basic imperatives that drive most architectural contests:

1. Good products are not enough. Products distribute architectures and can contribute to the success of an architectural strategy. However, as the case of Lotus suggests, good products alone are not enough. But if the sponsor invests heavily in continuous product improvement, products of only modest capabilities can become the basis for architectural leadership. For example, both Zilog and AMD at various stages in the PC microprocessor contest made Intel-compatible chips that were superior to Intel's own; but neither company matched Intel's commitment to R&D, and both were left behind as Intel rolled out one generation of improved processor after another. Once an architecture is established, it in turn becomes a distribution channel for additional products, with the architectural controller's products holding the favored position.

2. Implementations matter. Manufacturing decisions are playing an increasingly important role in product strategy. But since successful architectures have a high design content and usually a high software content, manufacturing skills by themselves are not sufficient to prevail in architectural competition. Japanese and other Asian companies, for example, despite their great manufacturing prowess, have only rarely established architectural franchises. Generally, they have settled for positions as clone makers or commodity implementors. Perhaps the only area where Japanese companies have established proprietary control over an important architectural space is in video games. But even the leaders in this arena, Nintendo and Sega, are at risk. (See "Scenarios for Architectural Competition: Video Games" at the end of this article.)

While insufficient on their own, however, manufacturing skills may well be an essential competence for success in the architectural contests of the 1990s. The reason: implementation is increasingly becoming the key to winning architectural control. In microprocessors, for example, a good implementation can improve performance by a factor of two. That's why architectural leaders like Intel typically make their own chips. By contrast, Sun Microsystems has chosen to focus solely on the design of its SPARC microprocessor, a decision that has been a source of recent difficulty for the company because subpar supplier implementations have compromised SPARC performance. High-quality implementations are equally important in the new generations of hand-held computers. Indeed, the more advanced information technology makes inroads into consumer markets, the more manufacturing skills will prove invaluable.

Manufacturing skills may well be essential for success in architectural contests.

3. Successful architectures are proprietary, but open. Closed architectures do not win broad franchises. Choosing the right degree of openness is one of the most subtle and difficult decisions in architectural contests. IBM opened its PC architecture too broadly—it should have, and could have, retained control of either or both the operating system and microprocessor standard.

Apple made the opposite mistake of bundling the Mac operating system too closely to its own hardware. Sun, in contrast to Apple, opened its SPARC RISC architec-

Architectures that cannot evolve to occupy an ever-broader competitive space are dead ends.

ture very early, both to software developers and processor cloners; it has the lead position in workstations, and its broad base of third-party software support has helped maintain customer loyalty though a series of technical stumbles. Autodesk's computer-aided design (CAD) software for builders is open to add-on third-party packages, like kitchen design tools, and its broad base of supporting software has given it control of a small but very profitable franchise.

4. General-purpose architectures absorb special-purpose solutions. Architectures that cannot evolve to occupy an ever-broader competitive space are dead ends. Wang's lucrative word processor franchise was absorbed by general-purpose PCs. Special-purpose CAD workstations from Daisy, Applicon, and others were absorbed by more general-purpose desktop machines. Special-purpose game machines will, in all likelihood, be absorbed by more general-purpose consumer systems.

5. Low-end systems swallow high-end systems. Minicomputers poached away huge chunks of mainframe territory and were assaulted in turn by workstations and networks. Workstations are under pressure by increasingly high performance PCs. Traditional supercomputers and very high-end mainframes are vulnerable to parallel arrays of inexpensive microprocessors. High-end data-storage systems are similarly under attack from arrays of inexpensive, redundant disks. Although IBM helped create the personal computer revolution, it steadfastly refused to recognize its implications. Until relatively recently, it even called its desktop products division "Entry Systems," ignoring the fact that today's microprocessor-based machines are a replacement for traditional computers, not an entry point or way station to them.

However, managers must keep in mind that even those companies that best follow these principles are not necessarily guaranteed continued success in the marketplace. Architectural contests typically move through a number of different phases, and only those companies that successfully navigate them all, maintaining their pace and direction in the fluid environment of rapidly evolving technologies, emerge as winners over the long term. It's a delicate balancing act, and one that requires ever-increasing flexibility as the technologies mature.

There are five principal phases to architectural competition:

Commitment. Architectural challenges usually emerge from the early-stage chaos of competing point products. Before the IBM PC, personal computers were rigid, closed systems that tended to bundle their own operating systems and applications software. Compaq had the insight that by purchasing a Microsoft operating system identical to that of the PC, it could ride the wave of the PC's success. Microsoft then insisted that all subsequent clone makers buy the same operating system and so seized the critical PC software architectural standard. Microsoft's insight was to realize that it was in an architectural contest and to take the appropriate steps, including steadily expanding the generality and scope of its systems to come out the winner.

Diffusion. Large profits come from broad franchises. Open architectures are successful because they can be broadly diffused. Xerox's Interpress page-description software, which converts digital data into printer instructions, is excellent but can be purchased only with Xerox high-end printers. Adobe, by contrast, has widely licensed its PostScript language and has become the industry standard setter. Intel widely licensed the early versions of its xx86 processors, then sharply restricted licensing of its 386 chip after the Intel standard had become firmly entrenched. IBM, on the other hand, has long resisted diffusing its mainframe and minicomputer software.

Of course, diffusion decisions are not without risk. Once again, balance and timing are essential. For example, Philips licensed its compact disc technology to Sony to increase market penetration. But Sony outperformed Philips and took half the market. Philips's standard was a static one that it never developed further.

Lock-in. A company has a "lock" on an architecture when competitors are trained to wait until the architectural leader introduces each new product generation. Intel and Microsoft, at least temporarily, seem to have achieved this position in PC markets. Sun was on the verge of a locked-in franchise in workstations but may have fallen short; the performance of its SPARC RISC processor design has been lagging behind the competition, and the company neglected to solidify its franchise by moving rapidly down to lower end platforms.

But lock-in is sustainable only when a company aggressively and continuously cannibalizes its own product line and continually and compatibly extends the architecture itself. This is a strategic choice that many companies find difficult to make. Often, managers become overprotective of the products that brought them their original success. IBM, for example, has frittered away a powerful lock on back-office transaction processing and operating systems. In a misguided effort to protect hardware sales, it has refused to release products, long since developed internally, that would adapt its best-selling AS400 minicomputer software to the RS6000 workstation. Such reflexive self-protection simply hands over a valuable franchise to the Microsofts and other vendors storming up from the low end.

Though painful, it is absolutely necessary to cannibalize old architectures.

Harvest. Of course, the ultimate objective of architectural competition is to win a market leader's share of the profits. Just to give one dramatic example, profit margins on Intel's xx86 family of chips are in the 40% to 50% range and account for well over 100% of the company's earnings. But no locked-in position is ever completely safe, and companies must be careful when they harvest not to rest on their previous successes. Indeed, Intel may have harvested too aggressively, drawing out spirited recent attacks by clone makers such as AMD and Cyrix.

Obsolescence and **Regeneration.** Just as products must be cannibalized, so must architectures themselves. The better the architecture, the longer its lifespan; but sooner or later every architecture, no matter how well designed, becomes obsolete. And before it does, the market leader must be prepared to move ahead, to do away with the old and introduce the new. Industry leaders often fail to cannibalize their old architectures, but although nothing is more painful, to do so is absolutely necessary. Otherwise, competitors quickly move to create and introduce rival franchises, and these eventually dominate the industry. IBM's failure to cannibalize its mainframe and minicomputer franchises provides a stark example of the catastrophic effects of waiting too long.

DEC provides another example. The company developed outstanding RISC products very early. But DEC declined to cannibalize its profitable VAX-VMS architecture because its VMS operating system, the source of its franchise, was tightly integrated with its aging VAX hardware. Predictably, DEC was beaten out by vendors such as Sun Microsystems and Microsoft, which didn't hesitate to move in with their newer, more powerful alternatives. (The main developer of DEC's advanced systems, Dave Cutler, is now in charge of developing NT for Microsoft.)

There are three lessons here. First, with better architecture DEC could have kept VMS alive longer. If VMS had been "portable," that is, not restricted to VAX hardware, DEC could have ported VMS to other vendors' hardware, making VMS an industry standard. Indeed, the company could have used RISC technology itself without losing its VMS franchise. Second, DEC would have been better off cannibalizing itself, rather than waiting to be cannibalized by others.

The third lesson, though, is the most important. As DEC's experiences with VMS and IBM's mistakes with the mainframe and minicomputer franchises show, the cultural and organizational structures useful for managing traditional, closed, integrated businesses will not work for companies that intend to compete with architectural strategy. In fact, we believe that architectural competition is stimulating the development of a new form of business organization.

This new structure, which we call the Silicon Valley Model, has major implications both for information technology and for many other industries. The model is still young and rapidly changing, and although Microsoft probably comes closest, no company fits it perfectly.

Managing Architectural Competition: The Silicon Valley Model

The Silicon Valley Model arose a decade ago when early architectural competitors noticed that they faced the same problems in managing organizations that they faced with technologies and architectural strategies.

In retrospect, this is not surprising. Architecture responds to the same imperatives in both systems and organizations. It reduces complexity. It permits clean separation between centralized general-purpose functions and decentralized or specialized functions. It enables management of unpredictability and change; individual technologies, components, or products can be switched without the need to redo everything. For similar reasons, good architecture facilitates experimentation and competition: once the framework is specified, multiple approaches can compete without jeopardizing compatibility. And finally, a standard architecture permits many systems and organizations to be developed independently and still work together gracefully. (See "Scenarios for Architectural Competition: Page- and Image-Description Standards" at the end of this article.)

As an organizational paradigm, the Silicon Valley Model therefore has several characteristic features and advantages. Following are the most important:

1. Organizational architecture and decision making that mirror technical architecture. Any organization should develop and use good technical architectures. But Silicon Valley Model firms take an additional step: the structure of the firm itself mirrors the technical architectures it uses.

Thus, for example, Microsoft is structured so that its existing systems software and applications software are managed separately, as are new architectural efforts such as NT. In this manner, Microsoft can diffuse its applications across multiple operating systems (both its own and others, like the Apple Macintosh), while also marketing its operating systems by courting other vendors' applications. The two businesses can work largely independently, yet only Microsoft gains the benefits of their synergism. Most decisions can be made directly within the organization responsible for the relevant architectural domain; this minimizes complex vertical and horizontal debates.

2. Meritocracy and direct feedback. Silicon Valley Model firms enable and force direct performance feedback, at levels ranging from individuals to business units. At Microsoft, team members rate each other periodically in peer reviews. Outstanding performers are rewarded; laggards are warned, then fired. Technical expertise is required for a large fraction of senior management, and communication occurs directly between the relevant parties, unbuffered by hierarchy.

By contrast, performance ratings in traditional bureaucracies are determined by managers at higher levels, and compensation is rarely based on long-term corporate performance. The process is often heavily politicized; dissent is suppressed, and incompetence goes unpunished.

Architectural competition also exposes Silicon Valley Model firms to another form of peer review—product competition. To succeed as industry standard setters, firms must license their architectures to competitors, while also developing critical products themselves. As a result, each layer of the firm (and of the architecture) is exposed to direct competition and market feedback. Hence although Microsoft controls Windows, application groups still compete individually: Excel against Lotus and QuattroPro, Word against Word-Perfect and AmiPro, and so forth. Architectural leadership provides an advantage, but prevents a cover-up. Silicon Valley Model firms are structured so that excellence is the only defense.

Silicon Valley Model firms take an additonal step: The structure of the firm itself mirrors the technical architectures it uses.

3. Clean boundaries, both internal and external. In architected corporate structures, organizations can create and dissolve alliances rapidly, both internally and externally. Organizations are very flat, and development groups have simple, clean interfaces to each other determined by architectural boundaries. Architecture and point products can be kept apart. Moreover, products can invisibly incorporate architected "engines" developed by other organizations, including competitors. For example, a start-up called InfoNow has organized alliances involving itself, Microsoft, publishers, computer vendors, and other software companies. InfoNow packages software products, together with reviews and samples of them, which are preloaded for free on computers; the software products, however, are encrypted. Users can sample them, read reviews, and then purchase them by telephone, which triggers electronic decryption. Adding new software packages is trivial.

4. Internal proprietary control of architecture and critical implementations, externalized commodities and niches. Silicon Valley Model firms seek to externalize the maximum possible fraction of their total system, while carefully controlling those areas required to establish and hold an architectural franchise. Thus core development of the general purpose architecture is always internally controlled. So usually are critical product implementations, which cover the broadest markets and are required either for early diffusion or later harvesting. Silicon Valley firms also carefully manage their dependencies, so as not to become unilaterally dependent on architectural competitors.

Broad, cost-sensitive markets are the strategic high ground, if covered by proprietary architectures.

On balance, however, Silicon Valley Model firms are much less autarkic than traditional large firms. Niche products, commodity components, and architectures controlled by others are outsourced, and/or relegated to licensees. In fact, Silicon Valley firms actively seek to commoditize regions not under their control.

This yields several benefits. For one, companies can focus on what they do best and on the efforts critical to architectural success. For another, broad outsourcing and licensing create competition among suppliers and licensees, which broadens the market and benefits the architectural leader. PC price wars delight Intel, Microsoft, and Novell; IBM and Compaq take the heat.

Interestingly, this contradicts the 1980s conventional wisdom that firms should avoid broad, cost-sensitive markets in favor of high-price niches. In fact, the broad market is the strategic high ground, if it is covered by a proprietary architecture. Niche product vendors can make profits, but they will remain minor players.

5. Migration and evolution over time. Just as architectures evolve and eventually become obsolete, so too with organizations. Thus the firm's internal structure and external alliances evolve along with its architecture and market position. As new layers are added to an existing architectural position (Windows on top of DOS, then NT underneath Windows), new organizations are created; a similar situation occurs when an architecture must be cannibalized. Some Silicon Valley Model firms will soon face cannibalization; it will be interesting to see how they do.

Broader Implications of the Silicon Valley Model

The Silicon Valley Model is very much a product of a few companies in the computer sector, just as mass production was invented by Ford and just-in-time production by Toyota. And as in those cases, we believe that the Silicon Valley Model will diffuse throughout the broader information technology sector as the computer, telecommunications, information services, and consumer electronics industries merge.

In addition, however, as industrial competition in all industries becomes more complex and technological change accelerates, the model may have important effects upon many other fields. We think that it provides a framework that allows proprietary leaders in general to have the greatest span of control and profitability with the least complexity and smallest size. In fact, we think that the model is appropriate for small and large companies alike; it does, however, penalize unnecessary size. (Microsoft, with fewer than 15,000 employees, has a market capitalization equal to IBM's.) We will therefore close with an example of how architectural strategy and the Silicon Valley Model could have been used more than a decade ago, by Xerox.

Xerox became a large, global company through a single proprietary technology—xerography. Xerographic "marking engines" are the core of photocopiers, printers, and facsimile machines, all of which Xerox invented. But Xerox chose to exploit its control of xerography using the traditional strategy of integrated companies.

Where Xerox felt it could not develop products profitably itself, it simply left the market vacant. As a result, when the company's patent position eroded, Japanese competitors took the bulk of the blossoming low-end markets for personal copiers, laser printers, and fax machines. Xerox's market share declined from nearly 100% to about 30%.

Instead, Xerox could have developed an architecture for a broad family of machines and control systems, including interfaces for scanners, document handlers, and "finishers" for collating, stapling, and binding. It could have licensed its technology to other firms, and/or sold them xerographic engines. It could have developed products for core markets, leaving others to niche companies.

Every few years, the company could have changed or enhanced its architectures to improve its products and competitive position. The result could have been a Microsoft-like position, with Xerox holding the lion's share of the profits in a highly competitive, dynamic market—yet one under its own effective control. We think that similar strategies are available to companies in other complex industries—aerospace and machine tools, among others. If so, the information sector's strategic and organizational innovations might prove as interesting as its technology.

Scenarios for Architectural Competition: Graphical User Interfaces

GRAPHICAL USER INTERFACES (GUIs) are the software that permits users to maneuver around applications visually—for example, issuing commands by pointing to icons—providing a simple, consistent method of working with many different programs. The evolution of the GUI market provides a dramatic example of the dynamics of architectural competition.

The original GUI was developed at Xerox's famed Palo Alto Research Center (PARC) and unveiled with the Xerox Star in the early 1980s. The Star was a brilliant achievement for its time—a high-performance, if very expensive, easy-to-use networked workstation. But it was a completely closed system; there was no published applications-program interface, so no one but Xerox could supply software to run on the Star. Its appeal was therefore far too limited ever to become a pervasive desktop standard.

Steve Jobs adapted the Star technology to Apple, but it took several tries before Apple began to make inroads in the GUI arena. Apple's first try was the Lisa, a substantially closed system that failed to attract any market share. The company got it more nearly right with the Macintosh. At least in later incarnations, the Mac has been hospitable to third-party software developers. It is considerably less expensive than the Lisa and has a superb operating system/GUI architecture. But Apple has still sharply limited its distribution potential by insisting on bundling its architecture with only its own, second-rate hardware. The Mac is hardly a failure, but had Apple licensed its systems software broadly, Apple and its microprocessor partner, Motorola, could have exercised the same architectural control over personal computing that Microsoft and Intel do now.

The operating system/GUI architectural struggle is far from over and will be one of the most heated competitive arenas of the 1990s. IBM OS/2 2.0 is technically excellent but suffers from a very late start; Microsoft's brand new NT system, which will run Windows applications, will raise the hurdles yet again. A variety of UNIX-based standards are alternatives to systems derived from the original DOS. And IBM and Apple have joined forces on a next-generation operating system/GUI in their Taligent partnership.

As the ongoing GUI contest suggests, architectural battles are fast-moving, hotly challenged, and rarely completely settled. The rewards to a winner, however, can be great.

Scenarios for Architectural Competition: Video Games

THE HOME VIDEO GAME industry, dominated by Nintendo and Sega, is a serious industry. Some 30 million American homes, or about 70% of all homes with a child between the ages of eight and twelve, own a video game. Both Nintendo and Sega sell video game consoles (basic, 16-bit, 286-level computers) with tightly bundled operating systems. Game software is developed by independent vendors under tightly controlled licenses but distributed only through the two companies' networks at hefty markups. Profits flow from game sales, not consoles.

Bundled architectures are ripe for attack by more open systems, just as the Apple II was overwhelmed by the IBM PC. In fact, a number of American companies have targeted the game market. Electronic Arts, for one, has won a copyright suit allowing it to reverse-engineer Sega's operating system. The availability of a Sega system clone would break that company's hold over game software and open up console manufacturing to cloners. Another company, 3DO (formerly the San Mateo Software Group), has plans to release a powerful consumer-oriented operating system that will be ideally suited for games. Specifications have been provided to a number of Asian manufacturers including Matsushita, a 3DO investor, for a CD-ROM-based console. Existing best-selling games, presumably, could readily be adapted to the new system; 3DO's objective is to own a Windows-like architectural franchise in the consumer world.

An interesting and potentially formidable dark-horse competitor is Silicon Graphics, a company that has built its industry-leading three-dimensional image manipulation technology into a billion-dollar business. From its original base in the engineering CAD industry, Silicon Graphics has found a new niche supplying the technology behind the spectacular special effects in Hollywood hits like "Terminator II." These systems could produce mind-boggling game effects; Silicon Graphics is known to have a consumer/game strategy underway.

All these companies have ambitions that extend well beyond toys. Games may be just the first of a series of image-oriented consumer platforms for everything from news services, home shopping, or endless entertainment services. On the principle that the low end always wins, such platforms eventually may supplant the current generation of personal computers. Microsoft and Intel beware.

Scenarios for Architectural Competition: Page- and Image-Description Standards

PAGE- AND IMAGE-DESCRIPTION standards are rapidly evolving from their initial base in printers into a very large business that will transform the entire printing and publishing industry. Probably most published material is now captured in electronic format, and a major competition is shaping up for control of the standard for storage, transmission, and manipulation of complex text, images, and multimedia documents. The technology involved is extraordinarily sophisticated and processing-intensive. Data compression and decompression and image-manipulation algorithms tax all but the very fastest of available processors; data storage requirements are very large; and requirements for communications capacity outpace most conventional systems. All these hurdles are falling very rapidly before a wide range of technical advances.

At the moment, Adobe must be considered the front-runner in the standards contest. Its Acrobat product, due to be introduced this year, will provide the industry's most advanced storage, compression, and transmission capabilities. The first versions will permit users to annotate, but not edit, electronically stored texts. Later releases are expected to include editing options. Microsoft is mounting a major challenge, at least in the word processing of documents and fonts. The dark horse is Xerox, which traditionally has possessed a vast array of image- and text-oriented technologies that it somehow never manages to commercialize. A number of smaller companies have also planted their pennants, including, refreshingly, two from Europe, Harlequin and Hyphen. Hewlett-Packard and Microsoft have formed an alliance to stay in contention, but their solutions are, for the moment at least, quite limited.

An early inning in the contest will involve the possibility of creating a new proprietary fax standard. The combination of faxes with high-quality plain paper printers could induce a very substantial increase in fax usage, particularly if images are of sufficiently high quality to transmit pictures, working drawings, and the like. Two new products, PostScript for Fax from Adobe and Satisfaxion from Intel, provide much improved resolution and decrease the required data compression to allow existing low-capacity communication systems to handle complex images. Both interconnect with standard fax machines to send and receive low-resolution images.

Originally published in March–April 1993
Reprint 93203

Increasing Returns and the New World of Business

W. BRIAN ARTHUR

Executive Summary

OUR UNDERSTANDING of how markets and businesses operate was passed down to us more than a century ago by English economist Alfred Marshall. It is based on the assumption of diminishing returns: products or companies that get ahead in a market eventually run into limitations so that a predictable equilibrium of prices and market shares is reached. The theory was valid for the bulk-processing, smokestack economy of Marshall's day. But in this century, Western economies have gone from processing resources to processing information, from the application of raw energy to the application of ideas. The mechanisms that determine economic behavior have also shifted—from diminishing returns to increasing returns.

Increasing returns are the tendency for that which is ahead to get further ahead and for that which is losing advantage to lose further advantage. If a product gets ahead, increasing returns can magnify the advantage, and the product can go on to lock in the market.

Mechanisms of increasing returns exist alongside those of diminishing returns in all industries. But, in general, diminishing returns hold sway in the traditional, resource-processing industries. Increasing returns reign in the newer, knowledge-based industries. Modern economies have split into two interrelated worlds of business corresponding to the tow types of returns. The two worlds have different economics. They differ in behavior, style, and culture. They call for different management techniques, strategies, and codes of government regulation.

The author illuminates those differences by explaining how increasing returns operate in high tech and in service industries. He also offers advice to managers in knowledge-based markets.

OUR UNDERSTANDING of how markets and businesses operate was passed down to us more than a century ago by a handful of European economists— Alfred Marshall in England and a few of his contemporaries on the continent. It is an understanding based squarely upon the assumption of diminishing returns: products or companies that get ahead in a market eventually run into limitations, so that a predictable equilibrium of prices and market shares is reached. The theory was roughly valid for the bulk-processing, smokestack economy of Marshall's day. And it still thrives in today's economics textbooks. But steadily and continuously in this century, Western economies have undergone a transformation from bulk-material manufacturing to design and use of technology—from processing of resources to processing of information, from application of raw energy to application of ideas. As this shift has occurred, the underlying mechanisms that determine economic behavior have shifted from ones of diminishing to ones of *increasing* returns.

Increasing returns are the tendency for that which is ahead to get further ahead, for that which loses advantage to lose further advantage. They are mechanisms of positive feedback that operate—within markets, businesses, and industries—to reinforce that which gains success or aggravate that which suffers loss. Increasing returns generate not equilibrium but instability: If a product or a company or a technology—one of many competing in a market—gets ahead by chance or clever strategy, increasing returns can magnify this advantage, and the product or company or technology can go on to lock in the market. More than causing products to become standards, increasing returns cause businesses to work differently, and they stand many of our notions of how business operates on their head.

Mechanisms of increasing returns exist alongside those of diminishing returns in all industries. But roughly speaking, diminishing returns hold sway in the traditional part of the economy—the processing industries. Increasing returns reign in the newer part—the knowledge-based industries. Modern economies have therefore bifurcated into two interrelated worlds of business corresponding to the two types of returns. The two worlds have different economics. They differ in behavior, style, and culture. They call for different management techniques, strategies, and codes of government regulation.

They call for different understandings.

Alfred Marshall's World

Let's go back to beginnings—to the diminishing-returns
view of Alfred Marshall and his contemporaries. Marshall's world of the 1880s and 1890s was one of bulk production: of metal ores, aniline dyes, pig iron, coal, lum-
ber, heavy chemicals, soybeans, coffee—commodities
heavy on resources, light on know-how. In that world it
was reasonable to suppose, for example, that if a coffee
plantation expanded production it would ultimately be
driven to use land less suitable for coffee. In other
words, it would run into diminishing returns. So if coffee
plantations competed, each one would expand until it
ran into limitations in the form of rising costs or diminishing profits. The market would be shared by many
plantations, and a market price would be established at
a predictable level—depending on tastes for coffee and
the availability of suitable farmland. Planters would produce coffee so long as doing so was profitable, but
because the price would be squeezed down to the average cost of production, no one would be able to make a
killing. Marshall said such a market was in perfect competition, and the economic world he envisaged fitted
beautifully with the Victorian values of his time. It was
at equilibrium and therefore orderly, predictable and
therefore amenable to scientific analysis, stable and
therefore safe, slow to change and therefore continuous.
Not too rushed, not too profitable. In a word, mannerly.
In a word, genteel.

With a few changes, Marshall's world lives on a century later within that part of the modern economy still
devoted to bulk processing: of grains, livestock, heavy
chemicals, metals and ores, foodstuffs, retail goods—the
part where operations are largely repetitive day to day or

week to week. Product differentiation and brand names now mean that a few companies rather than many compete in a given market. But typically, if these companies try to expand, they run into some limitation: in numbers of consumers who prefer their brand, in regional demand, in access to raw materials. So no company can corner the market. And because such products are normally substitutable for one another, something like a standard price emerges. Margins are thin and nobody makes a killing. This isn't exactly Marshall's perfect competition, but it approximates it.

The Increasing-Returns World

What would happen if Marshall's diminishing returns were reversed so that there were *increasing* returns? If products that got ahead thereby got further ahead, how would markets work?

Let's look at the market for operating systems for personal computers in the early 1980s when CP/M, DOS, and Apple's Macintosh systems were competing. Operating systems show increasing returns: if one system gets ahead, it attracts further software developers and hardware manufacturers to adopt it, which helps it get further ahead. CP/M was first in the market and by 1979 was well established. The Mac arrived later, but it was wonderfully easy to use. DOS was born when Microsoft locked up a deal in 1980 to supply an operat-

In 1939, English economist John Hicks warned that admitting increasing returns would lead to "the wreckage of the greater part of economic theory." But Hicks had it wrong.

ing system for the IBM PC. For a year or two, it was by
no means clear which system would prevail. The new
IBM PC—DOS's platform—was a kludge. But the growing base of DOS/IBM users encouraged software developers such as Lotus to write for DOS. DOS's prevalence—and the IBM PC's—bred further prevalence, and
eventually the DOS/IBM combination came to dominate
a considerable portion of the market. That history is
now well known. But notice several things: It was not
predictable in advance (before the IBM deal) which system would come to dominate. Once DOS/IBM got
ahead, it locked in the market because it did not pay for
users to switch. The dominant system was not the best:
DOS was derided by computer professionals. And once
DOS locked in the market, its sponsor, Microsoft, was
able to spread its costs over a large base of users. The
company enjoyed killer margins.

These properties, then, have become the hallmarks of
increasing returns: market instability (the market tilts to
favor a product that gets ahead), multiple potential outcomes (under different events in history, different operating systems could have won), unpredictability, the
ability to lock in a market, the possible predominance of
an inferior product, and fat profits for the winner. They
surprised me when I first perceived them in the late
1970s. They were also repulsive to economists brought
up on the order, predictability, and optimality of Marshall's world. Glimpsing some of these properties in
1939, English economist John Hicks warned that admitting increasing returns would lead to "the wreckage of
the greater part of economic theory." But Hicks had it
wrong: the theory of increasing returns does not destroy
the standard theory—it complements it. Hicks felt
repugnance not just because of unsavory properties but

also because in his day no mathematical apparatus existed to analyze increasing-returns markets. That situation has now changed. Using sophisticated techniques from qualitative dynamics and probability theory, I and others have developed methods to analyze increasing-returns markets. The theory of increasing returns is new, but it already is well established. And it renders such markets amenable to economic understanding.

In the early days of my work on increasing returns, I was told they were an anomaly. Like some exotic particle in physics, they might exist in theory but would be rare in practice. And if they did exist, they would last for only a few seconds before being arbitraged away. But by the mid-1980s, I realized increasing returns were neither rare nor ephemeral. In fact, a major part of the economy was subject to increasing returns—high technology.

Why should this be so? There are several reasons:

Up-front costs. High-tech products—pharmaceuticals, computer hardware and software, aircraft and missiles, telecommunications equipment, bioengineered drugs, and suchlike—are by definition complicated to design and to deliver to the marketplace. They are heavy on know-how and light on resources. Hence they typically have R&D costs that are large relative to their unit production costs. The first disk of Windows to go out the door cost Microsoft $50 million; the second and subsequent disks cost $3. Unit costs fall as sales increase.

Network effects. Many high-tech products need to be compatible with a network of users. So if much downloadable software on the Internet will soon appear as programs written in Sun Microsystems' Java language, users will need Java on their computers to run them. Java has competitors. But the more it gains prevalence, the more likely it will emerge as a standard.

Customer groove-in. High-tech products are typically difficult to use. They require training. Once users invest in this training—say, the maintenance and piloting of Airbus passenger aircraft—they merely need to update these skills for subsequent versions of the product. As more market is captured, it becomes easier to capture future markets.

In high-tech markets, such mechanisms ensure that products that gain market advantage stand to gain further advantage, making these markets unstable and subject to lock-in. Of course, lock-in is not forever. Technology comes in waves, and a lock-in such as DOS's can last only as long as a particular wave lasts.

So we can usefully think of two economic regimes or worlds: a bulk-production world yielding products that essentially are congealed resources with a little knowledge and operating according to Marshall's principles of diminishing returns, and a knowledge-based part of the economy yielding products that essentially are congealed knowledge with a little resources and operating under increasing returns. The two worlds are not neatly split. Hewlett-Packard, for example, designs knowledge-based devices in Palo Alto, California, and manufactures them in bulk in places like Corvallis, Oregon, or Greeley, Colorado. Most high-tech companies have both knowledge-based operations and

Some products—like the IBM PC—start in the increasing-returns world but later in their life cycle become virtual commodities that belong to Marshall's processing world.

bulk-processing operations. But because the rules of the game differ for each, companies often separate them—as Hewlett-Packard does. Conversely, manufacturing companies have operations such as logistics, branding, marketing, and distribution, which belong largely to the knowledge world. And some products—like the IBM PC—start in the increasing-returns world but later in their life cycle become virtual commodities that belong to Marshall's processing world.

The Halls of Production and the Casino of Technology

Because the two worlds of business—processing bulk goods and crafting knowledge into products—differ in their underlying economics, it follows that they differ in their character of competition and their culture of management. It is a mistake to think that what works in one world is appropriate for the other.

There is much talk these days about a new management style that involves flat hierarchies, mission orientation, flexibility in strategy, market positioning, reinvention, restructuring, reengineering, repositioning, reorganization, and re-everything else. Are these new insights or are they fads? Are they appropriate for all organizations? Why are we seeing this new management style?

Let us look at the two cultures of competition. In bulk processing, a set of standard prices typically emerges. Production tends to be repetitive—much the same from day to day or even from year to year. Competing therefore means keeping product flowing, trying to improve quality, getting costs down. There is an art to this sort of management, one widely discussed in the literature. It favors an environment free of surprises or glitches—an environment characterized by control and planning. Such an environment requires not just people to carry out production but also people to plan and control it. So it favors a hierarchy of bosses and workers. Because bulk processing is repetitive, it allows constant improvement, constant optimization. And so, Marshall's world tends to be one that favors hierarchy, planning, and controls. Above all, it is a world of optimization.

Competition is different in knowledge-based industries because the economics are different. If knowledge-based companies are competing in winner-take-most markets, then managing becomes redefined as a series of quests for the next technological winner—the next cash cow. The goal becomes the search for the Next Big Thing. In this milieu, management becomes not production oriented but mission oriented. Hierarchies flatten not because democracy is suddenly bestowed on the workforce or because computers can cut out much of middle management. They flatten because, to be effective, the deliverers of the next-thing-for-the-company need to be organized like commando units in small teams that report directly to the CEO or to the board. Such people need free rein. The company's future survival depends upon them. So they—and the commando teams that report to them in turn—will be treated not as employees but as equals in the business of the company's success. Hierarchy dissipates and dissolves.

Does this mean that hierarchy should disappear in meatpacking, steel production, or the navy? Contrary to recent management evangelizing, a style that is called for in Silicon Valley will not necessarily be appropriate in the processing world. An aircraft's safe arrival depends on the captain, not on the flight attendants.

The cabin crew can usefully be "empowered" and treated as human beings. This approach is wise and proper. But forever there will be a distinction—a hierarchy—between cockpit and cabin crews.

In fact, the style in the diminishing-returns Halls of Production is much like that of a sophisticated modern factory: the goal is to keep high-quality product flowing at low cost. There is little need to watch the market every day, and when things are going smoothly the tempo can be leisurely. By contrast, the style of competition in the increasing-returns arena is more like gambling. Not poker, where the game is static and the players vie for a succession of pots. It is casino gambling, where part of the game is to choose which games to play, as well as playing them with skill. We can imagine the top figures in high tech—the Gateses and Gerstners and Groves of their industries—as milling in a large casino. Over at this table, a game is starting called multimedia. Over at that one, a game called Web services. In the corner is electronic banking. There are many such tables. You sit at one. How much to play? you ask. Three billion, the croupier replies. Who'll be playing? We won't know until they show up. What are the rules? Those'll emerge as the game unfolds. What are my odds of winning? We can't say. Do you still want to play?

Adaptation means watching for the next wave and positioning the company to take advantage of it. Adaptation is what drives increasing-returns businesses, not optimization.

High technology, pursued at this level, is not for the timid.

In fact, the art of playing the tables in the Casino of Technology is primarily a psychological one. What counts to some degree—but only to some degree—is technical expertise, deep pockets, will, and courage. Above all, the rewards go to the players who are first to make sense of the new games looming out of the technological fog, to see their shape, to cognize them. Bill Gates is not so much a wizard of technology as a wizard of precognition, of discerning the shape of the next game.

We can now begin to see that the new style of management is not a fad. The knowledge-based part of the economy demands flat hierarchies, mission orientation, above all a sense of direction. Not five-year plans. We can also fathom the mystery of what I've alluded to as *re-everything*. Much of this "re-everything" predilection—in the bulk-processing world—is a fancy label for streamlining, computerizing, downsizing. However, in the increasing-returns world, especially in high tech, re-everything has become necessary because every time the quest changes, the company needs to change. It needs to reinvent its purpose, its goals, its way of doing things. In short, it needs to adapt. And adaptation never stops. In fact, in the increasing-returns environment I've just sketched, standard optimization makes little sense. You cannot optimize in the casino of increasing-returns games. You can be smart. You can be cunning. You can position. You can observe. But when the games themselves are not even fully defined, you cannot optimize. What you *can* do is adapt. Adaptation, in the proactive sense, means watching for the next wave that is coming, figuring out what shape it will take, and positioning the company to take advantage of it. Adaptation is what drives increasing-returns businesses, not optimization.

Playing the High-Tech Tables

Suppose you are a player in the knowledge-industry casino, in this increasing-returns world. What can you do to capitalize on the increasing returns at your disposal? How can you use them to capture markets? What strategic issues do you need to think about? In the processing world, strategy typically hinges upon capitalizing on core competencies, pricing competitively, getting costs down, bringing quality up. These are important also in the knowledge-based world, but so, too, are other strategies that make use of the special economics of positive feedbacks.

Two maxims are widely accepted in knowledge-based markets: it pays to hit the market first, and it pays to have superb technology. These maxims are true but do not guarantee success. Prodigy was first into the on-line services market but was passive in building its subscriber base to take advantage of increasing returns. As a result, it has fallen from its leading position and currently lags the other services. As for technology, Steve Jobs's NeXT workstation was superb. But it was launched into a market already dominated by Sun Microsystems and Hewlett-Packard. It failed. A new product often has to be two or three times better in some dimension—price, speed, convenience—to dislodge a locked-in rival. So in knowledge-based markets, entering first with a fine product can yield advantage. But as strategy, this is still too passive. What is needed is *active* management of increasing returns.

One active strategy is to discount heavily initially to build up an installed base. Netscape handed out its Internet browser for free and won 70% of its market.

Now it can profit from spin-off software and applications. Although such discounting is effective—and widely understood—it is not always implemented. Companies often err by pricing high initially to recoup expensive R&D costs. Yet even smart discounting to seed the market is ineffective unless the resulting installed base is exploited later. America Online built up a lead of more than 4.5 million subscribers by giving away free services. But because of the Internet's dominance, it is not yet clear whether it can transform this huge base into later profits.

Let's get a bit more sophisticated. Technological products do not stand alone. They depend on the existence of other products and other technologies. The Internet's World Wide Web operates within a grouping of businesses that include browsers, on-line news, E-mail, network retailing, and financial services. Pharmaceuticals exist within a network of physicians, testing labs, hospitals, and HMOs. Laser printers are part of a grouping of products that include computers, publishing software, scanners, and photo-input devices. Unlike products of the processing world, such as soybeans or rolled steel, technological products exist within local groupings of products that support and enhance them. They exist in mini-ecologies.

This interdependence has deep implications for strategy. When, in the mid-1980s, Novell introduced its network-operating system, NetWare, as a way of connecting personal computers in local networks, Novell made sure that NetWare was technically superior to its rivals. It also heavily discounted NetWare to build an installed base. But these tactics were not enough. Novell recognized that NetWare's success depended on attracting software applications to run on NetWare—which was a part of the ecology outside the company's control. So it set up incentives for software developers to write for NetWare rather than for its rivals. The software writers did just that. And by building NetWare's success, they ensured their own. Novell managed these cross-product positive feedbacks actively to lock in its market. It went on to profit hugely from upgrades, spin-offs, and applications of its own.

Another strategy that uses ecologies is linking and leveraging. This means transferring a user base built up upon one node of the ecology (one product) to neighboring nodes, or products. The strategy is very much like that in the game Go: you surround neighboring markets one by one, lever your user base onto them, and take them over—all the time enhancing your position in the industry. Microsoft levered its 60-million-person user base in DOS onto Windows, then onto Windows 95, and then onto Microsoft Network by offering inexpensive upgrades and by bundling applications. The strategy has been challenged legally. (See "In the Case of Microsoft . . ." at the end of this article.) But it recognizes that positive feedbacks apply across markets as well as within markets.

In fact, if technological ecologies are now the basic units for strategy in the knowledge-based world, players compete not by locking in a product on their own but by building *webs*—loose alliances of companies organized around a mini-ecology—that amplify positive feedbacks to the base technology. Apple, in closing its Macintosh system to outsiders in the 1980s, opted not to create such a web. It believed that with its superior technology, it could hold its increasing-returns market to itself. Apple indeed dominates its Mac-based ecology. But this ecology is now only 8% of the personal computer busi-

ness. IBM erred in the other direction. By passively
allowing other companies to join its PC web as clones,
IBM achieved a huge user base and locked in the market.
But the company itself wound up with a small share of
the spoils. The key in web building is active management of the cross-company mutual feedbacks. This
means making a careful choice of partners to build
upon. It also means that, rather than attempting to take
over all products in the ecology, dominant players in a
web should allow dependent players to lock in their
dependent products by piggybacking on the web's success. By thus ceding some of the profits, the dominant
players ensure that all participants remain committed to
the alliance.

Important also to strategy in knowledge-based markets is psychological positioning. Under increasing
returns, rivals will back off in a market not only if it is
locked in but if they *believe* it will be locked in by some-
one else. Hence we see psychological jockeying in the
form of preannouncements, feints, threatened alliances,
technological preening, touted future partnerships,
parades of vaporware (announced products that don't
yet exist). This posturing and puffing acts much the way
similar behavior does in a primate colony: it discourages
competitors from taking on a potentially dominant rival.
No moves need be made in this strategy of premarket
facedown. It is purely a matter of psychology.

What if you hold a losing hand? Sometimes it pays to
hold on for residual revenue. Sometimes a fix can be
provided by updated technology, fresh alliances, or product changes. But usually under heavy lock-in, these tactics do not work. The alternatives are then slow death or
graceful exit—relinquishing the field to concentrate on
positioning for the next technology wave. Exit may not

mean quitting the business entirely. America Online, CompuServe, Prodigy, and Microsoft Network have all ceded dominance of the on-line computer networking market to the Internet. But instead of exiting, they are steadily becoming adjuncts of the Net, supplying content services such as financial quotations or games and entertainment. They have lost the main game. But they will likely continue in a side game with its own competition for dominance within the Net's ecology.

Above all, strategy in the knowledge world requires CEOs to recognize that a different kind of economics is at work. CEOs need to understand which positive and negative feedback mechanisms are at play in the market ecologies in which they compete. Often there are several such mechanisms—interbraided, operating over different time frames, each needing to be understood, observed, and actively managed.

What about Service Industries?

So far, I've talked mainly about high tech. Where do service industries such as insurance, restaurants, and banking fit in? Which world do they belong to? The question is tricky. It would appear that such industries belong to the diminishing-returns, processing part of the economy because often there are regional limits to the demand for a given service, most services do consist of "processing" clients, and services are low-tech.

The truth is that network or user-base effects often operate in services. Certainly, retail franchises exist because of increasing returns. The more McDonald's restaurants or Motel 6 franchises are out there geographically, the better they are known. Such businesses are patronized not just for their quality but also because people want to know exactly what to expect. So the more prevalent they are, the more prevalent they can become. Similarly, the larger a bank's or insurance company's customer base, the more it can spread its fixed costs of headquarters staff, real estate, and computer operations. These industries, too, are subject to mild increasing returns.

So we can say more accurately that service industries are a hybrid. From day to day, they act like bulk-processing industries. But over the long term, increasing returns will dominate—even though their destabilizing effects are not as pronounced as in high tech. The U.S. airline business, for example, processes passengers day to day. So it seemed in 1981 that deregulation should enhance competition, as it normally does under diminishing returns. But over the long term, airlines in fact experience a positive feedback: under the hub-and-spoke system, once an airline gets into trouble, it cannot work the feeder system for its routes properly, its fleet ages, it starts a downward spiral, and it loses further routes. The result of deregulation over the long term has been a steady decline in large carriers, from 15 airlines in 1981 to approximately 6 at present. Some routes have become virtual monopolies, with resulting higher fares. None of this was intended. But it should have been predicted—given increasing returns.

In fact, the increasing-returns character of service industries is steadily strengthening. One of the marks of our time is that in services everything is going software—everything that is information based. So operations that were once handled by people—designing fancy financial instruments or automobiles or fashion goods, processing insurance claims, supplying and inventorying in retail, conducting paralegal searches for case precedents—are increasingly being handled by software. As this reengineering of services plays out, centralized software facilities come to the fore. Service providers become hitched into software networks, regional limitations weaken, and user-base network effects kick in.

This phenomenon can have two consequences. First, where the local character of service remains important, it can preserve a large number of service companies but clustered round a dominant software provider—like the large numbers of small, independent law firms tied in to the dominant computer-search network, Lexis-Nexis. Or physicians tied in to an HMO. Second, where locality is unimportant, network effects can transform competition toward the winner-take-most character we see in high tech. For example, when Internet-based retail banking arrives, regional demand limitations will vanish. Each virtual bank will gain in advantage as its network increases. Barring regulation, consumer banking will then become a contest among a few large banking networks. It will become an increasing-returns business.

Services belong to both the processing and the increasing-returns world. But their center of gravity is crossing over to the latter.

Thoughts for Managers

Where does all this leave us? At the beginning of this century, industrial economies were based largely on the bulk processing of resources. At the close of the century, they are based on the processing of resources *and* on the processing of knowledge. Economies have bifurcated into two worlds—intertwined, overlapping, and different. These two worlds operate under different economic principles. Marshall's world is characterized by planning, control, and hierarchy. It is a world of materials, of processing, of optimization. The increasing-returns world is characterized by observation, positioning, flattened organizations, missions, teams, and cunning. It is a world of psychology, of cognition, of adaptation.

Many managers have some intuitive grasp of this new increasing-returns world. Few understand it thoroughly. Here are some questions managers need to ask themselves when they operate in knowledge-based markets:

Do I understand the feedbacks in my market? In the processing world, understanding markets means understanding consumers' needs, distribution channels, and rivals' products. In the knowledge world, success requires a thorough understanding of the self-negating and self-reinforcing feedbacks in the market—the diminishing- and increasing-returns mechanisms. These feedbacks are interwoven and operate at different levels in the market and over different time frames.

Which ecologies am I in? Technologies exist not alone but in an interlinked web, or ecology. It is important to understand the ecologies a company's products belong to. Success or failure is often decided not just by the company but also by the success or failure of the web it belongs to. Active management of such a web can be an important magnifier of increasing returns.

Do I have the resources to play? Playing one of the increasing-returns games in the Casino of Technology requires several things: excellent technology, the ability to hit the market at the right time, deep pockets, strategic pricing, and a willingness to sacrifice current profits for future advantage. All this is a matter not just of resources but also of courage, resolution, will. And part of that resolution, that courage, is also the decisiveness to leave the market when increasing returns are moving against one. Hanging on to a losing position that is being further eroded by positive feedbacks requires throwing reinforcements into a battle already lost. Better to exit with financial dignity.

What games are coming next? Technology comes in successive waves. Those who have lost out on this wave can position for the next. Conversely, those who have made a killing on this cycle should not become complacent. The ability to profit under increasing returns is only as good as the ability to see what's coming in the next cycle and to position oneself for it—technologically, psychologically, and cooperatively. In high tech, it is as if we are moving slowly on a ship, with new technologies looming, taking shape, through a fog of unknowingness. Success goes to those who have the vision to foresee, to imagine, what shapes these next games will take.

These considerations appear daunting. But increasing-returns games provide large payoffs for those brave enough to play them and win. And they are exciting. Processing, in the service or manufacturing industries, has its own risks. Precisely because processing is low-margin, operations must struggle to stay afloat. Neither world of business is for the fainthearted.

In his book *Microcosm*, technology thinker George Gilder remarked, "The central event of the twentieth century is the overthrow of matter. In technology, economics, and the politics of nations, wealth in the form of physical resources is steadily declining in value and significance. The powers of mind are everywhere ascendant over the brute force of things." As the economy shifts steadily away from the brute force of things into the powers of mind, from resource-based bulk processing into knowledge-based design and reproduction, so it is shifting from a base of diminishing returns to one of increasing returns. A new economics—one very different from that in the textbooks—now applies, and nowhere is this more true than in high technology. Success will strongly favor those who understand this new way of thinking.

In the Case of Microsoft . . .

WHAT SHOULD BE LEGAL in this powerful and as yet unregulated world of increasing returns? What constitutes fair play? Should technology markets be regulated, and if so in what way? These questions have come to a head with the enormous amount of publicity generated by the U.S. Justice Department's current antitrust case against Microsoft.

In Marshall's world, antitrust regulation is well understood. Allowing a single player to control, say, more than 35% of the silver market is tantamount to allowing monopoly pricing, and the government rightly steps in. In the increasing-returns world, things are more complicated. There are arguments in favor of allowing a product or company in the web of technology to dominate a market, as well as arguments against. Consider these pros and cons:

Convenience. A locked-in product may provide a single standard of convenience. If a software company such as Microsoft allows us to double-click all the way from our computer screen straight to our bank account (by controlling all the technologies in between), this avoids a tedious balkanizing of standards, where we have to spend useless time getting into a succession of on-line connection products.

Fairness. If a product locks in because it is superior, this is fair, and it would be foolish to penalize such success. If it locks in merely because user base was levered over from a neighboring lock-in, this is unfair.

Technology Development. A locked-in product may obstruct technological advancement. If a clunker such as DOS locks up the PC market for ten years, there is little incentive for other companies to develop alternatives. The result is impeded technological progress.

Pricing. To lock in, a product usually has been discounted, and this established low price is often hard to raise. So monopoly pricing—of great concern in bulk-processing markets—is therefore rarely a major worry.

Added to these considerations, high tech is not a commodity industry. Dominance may consist not so much in cornering a single product as in successively taking over more and more threads of the web of technology, thereby preventing other players from getting access to new, breaking markets. It would be difficult to separate out each thread and to regulate it. And of course it may be impracticable to regulate a market before it forms—before it is even fully defined. There are no simple answers to antitrust regulation in the increasing-returns world. On balance, I would favor a high degree of regulatory restraint, with the addition of two key principles:

- **Do not penalize success.** Short-term monopolization of an increasing-returns market is correctly perceived as a reward or prize for innovation and risk taking. There is a temptation to single out dominant players and hit them with an antitrust suit. This reduces regulation to something like a brawl in an Old West saloon—if you see a head, hit it. Not a policy that preserves an incentive to innovate in the first place.

- **Don't allow head starts for the privileged.** This means that as a new market opens up—such as electronic consumer banking—companies that already dominate standards, operating systems, and neighboring technologies should not be allowed a ten-mile head start in the land rush that follows. All competitors should have fair and open access to the applicable technologies and standards.

  In practice, these principles would mean allowing the possibility of winner-take-all jackpots in each new subindustry, in each new wave of technology. But each contender should have access to whatever degree possible to the same technologies, the same open standards, so that all are lined up behind the same starting line. If industry does not make such provisions voluntarily, government regulation will impose them.

Originally published in July–August 1996
Reprint 96401

Building Effective R&D Capabilities Abroad

WALTER KUEMMERLE

Executive Summary

IN THE PAST, companies kept most of their research and development activities in their home country because they thought it important to have R&D close to where strategic decisions were being made. But today many companies choose to establish R&D networks in foreign countries in order to tap the knowledge there or to commercialize products for those markets at a competitive speed.

Adopting a global approach entails new, complex managerial challenges. It means linking R&D strategy to a company's overall business strategy. The first step in adopting such an approach is to build a team to lead the initiative—a team whose members are sufficiently senior to be able to mobilize resources at short notice. Second, companies must determine whether an R&D site's primary objective is to augment the expertise that

171

the home base has to offer to exploit that knowledge for use in the foreign country. That determination affects the choice of location and staff. For example, to augment the home base laboratory, a company would want to be near a foreign university; to exploit the home base laboratory, it would need to be near large markets and manufacturing facilities.

The best individual for managing both types of site combines the qualities of good scientist and good manager, knows how to integrate the new site with existing sites, understands technology trends, and is good at gaining access to foreign scientific communities.

As more pockets of knowledge emerge around the globe and competition in foreign markets mounts, only those companies that embrace and informed approach to global R&D will be able to meet the new challenges.

An INCREASING NUMBER of companies in technologically intensive industries such as pharmaceuticals and electronics have abandoned the traditional approach to managing research and development and are establishing global R&D networks in a noteworthy new way. For example, Canon is now carrying out R&D activities in 8 dedicated facilities in 5 countries, Motorola in 14 facilities in 7 countries, and Bristol-Myers Squibb in 12 facilities in 6 countries. In the past, most companies—even those with a considerable international presence in terms of sales and manufacturing—carried out the majority of their R&D activity in their home countries. Conventional wisdom held that strategy development and R&D had to be kept in close geographical proximity. Because strategic decisions were made primarily at corporate headquarters, the thinking went, R&D facilities should be close to home.

But such a centralized approach to R&D will no longer suffice—for two reasons. First, as more and more sources of potentially relevant knowledge emerge across the globe, companies must establish a presence at an increasing number of locations to access new knowledge and to absorb new research results from foreign universities and competitors into their own organizations. Second, companies competing around the world must move new products from development to market at an ever more rapid pace. Consequently, companies must build R&D networks that excel at tapping new centers of knowledge and at commercializing products in foreign markets with the speed required to remain competitive. And more and more, superior manufacturers are doing just that. (See the exhibit "Laboratory Sites Abroad in 1995.")

In an ongoing study on corporate strategy and the geographical dispersion of R&D sites, I have been examining the creation of global research networks by 32 U.S., Japanese, and European multinational companies.[1] The most successful companies in my study brought each new site's research productivity up to full speed within a few years and quickly transformed knowledge created there into innovative products. I found that establishing networks of such sites poses a number of new, complex managerial challenges. According to my research, managers of the most successful R&D networks understand the new dynamics of global R&D, link corporate strategy to R&D strategy, pick the appropriate sites, staff them

Laboratory Sites Abroad in 1995

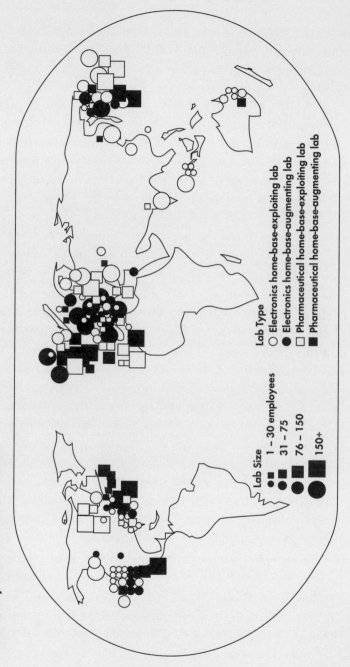

Lab Type
○ Electronics home-base-exploiting lab
● Electronics home-base-augmenting lab
□ Pharmaceutical home-base-exploiting lab
■ Pharmaceutical home-base-augmenting lab

Lab Size
1 – 30 employees
31 – 75
76 – 150
150+

with the right people, supervise the sites during start-up, and integrate the activities of the different foreign sites so that the entire network is a coordinated whole.

Adopting a Global Approach to R&D

Adopting a global approach to R&D requires linking R&D strategy to a company's overall business strategy. And that requires the involvement of managers at the highest levels of a company.

CREATING A TECHNOLOGY STEERING COMMITTEE

The first step in creating a global R&D network is to build a team that will lead the initiative. To establish a global R&D network, the CEOs and top-level managers of a number of successful companies that I studied assembled a small team of senior managers who had both technical expertise and in-depth organizational knowledge. The technology steering committees reported directly to the CEOs of their respective companies. They were generally small—five to eight members—and included managers with outstanding managerial and scientific records and a range of educational backgrounds and managerial responsibilities. The committees I studied included as members a former bench scientist who had transferred into manufacturing and had eventually become the head of manufacturing for the company's most important category of therapeutic drugs; a head of markting for memory chips who had worked before in product development in the same electronics company; and an engineer who had started out in product development, had moved to research, and eventually had become the vice president of R&D. Members of these committees were sufficiently senior to be able to mobilize resources at short notice; and they were actively involved in the management and supervision of R&D programs. In many cases, members included the heads of major existing R&D sites.

CATEGORIZING NEW R&D SITES

In selecting new sites, companies find it helpful first to articulate each site's primary objective. (See the exhibit "Establishing New R&D Sites.") R&D sites have one of two missions. The first type of site—what I call a *home-base-augmenting site*—is established in order to tap knowledge from competitors and universities around the globe; in that type of site, information *flows* from the foreign laboratory *to* the central lab at home. The second type of site—what I call a *home-base-exploiting site*—is established to support manufacturing facilities in foreign countries or to adapt standard products to the demand there; in that type of site, information flows *to* the foreign laboratory *from* the central lab at home. (See the exhibit "How Information Flows between Home-Base and Foreign R&D Sites.")

The overwhelming majority of the 238 foreign R&D sites I studied fell clearly into one of the two categories. Approximately 45% of all laboratory sites were home-base-augmenting sites, and 55% were home-base-exploiting sites. The two types of sites were of the same average size: about 100 employees. But they differed distinctly in their strategic purpose and leadership style.[2] (See "Home-Base-Augmenting and Home-Base-Exploiting Sites: Xerox and Eli Lilly" at the end of this article.)

Establishing New R&D Sites

Types of R&D Sites	Phase 1 Location Decision	Phase 2 Ramp-Up Period	Phase 3 Maximizing Lab Impact
Home-Base-Augmenting Laboratory Site Objective of establishment: absorbing knowledge from the local scientific community, creating new knowledge, and transferring it *to* the company's central R&D site	Select a location for its scientific excellence Promote cooperation between the company's senior scientists and managers	Choose as first laboratory leader a renowned local scientist with international experience—one who understands the dynamics of R&D at the new location Ensure enough critical mass	Ensure the laboratory's active participation in the local scientific community Exchange researchers with local university laboratories and with the home-base lab
Home-Base-Exploiting Laboratory Site Objective of establishment: commercializing knowledge by transferring it *from* the company's home base to the laboratory site abroad and from there to local manufacturing and marketing	Select a location for its proximity to the company's existing manufacturing and marketing locations Involve middle managers from other functional areas in start-up decisons	Choose as first laboratory leader an experienced product-development engineer with a strong companywide reputation, international experience, and knowledge of marketing and manufacturing	Emphasize smooth relations with the home-base lab Encourage employees to seek interaction with other corporate units beyond the manufacturing and marketing units that originally sponsored the lab

CHOOSING A LOCATION FOR THE SITE

Home-base-augmenting sites should be located in regional clusters of scientific excellence in order to tap new sources of knowledge. Central to the success of corporate R&D strategy is the ability of senior researchers to recognize and combine scientific advancements from different areas of science and technology. Absorbing the new knowledge can happen in a number of ways: through participation in formal or informal meeting circles that exist within a geographic area containing useful knowledge (a knowledge cluster), through hiring employees from competitors, or through sourcing laboratory equipment and research services from the same suppliers that competitors use.

For example, the Silicon Valley knowledge cluster boasts a large number of informal gatherings of experts as well as more formal ways for high-tech companies to exchange information with adjacent universities, such as

---

How Information Flows between Home-Base and Foreign R&D Sites

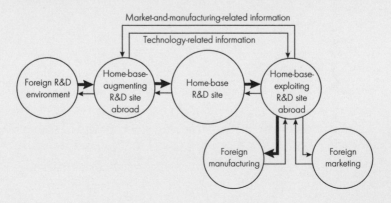

industrial liaison programs with Stanford University and the University of California at Berkeley. In the field of communication technology, Siemens, NEC, Matsushita, and Toshiba all operate laboratory sites near Princeton University and Bell Labs (now a part of Lucent Technologies) to take advantage of the expertise located there. For similar reasons, a number of companies in the same industry have established sites in the Kanto area surrounding Tokyo. Texas Instruments operates a facility in Tsukuba Science City, and Hewlett-Packard operates one in Tokyo.

After a company has picked and established its major R&D sites, it might want to branch out. It might selectively set up secondary sites when a leading competitor or a university succeeds in building a critical mass of research expertise in a more narrowly defined area of science and technology outside the primary cluster. In order to benefit from the resulting miniclusters of expertise, companies sometimes establish additional facilities. For that reason, NEC operates a small telecommunications-oriented R&D facility close to a university laboratory in London, and Canon operates an R&D facility in Rennes, France, close to one of France Telecom's major sites.

Home-base-exploiting sites, in contrast, should be located close to large markets and manufacturing facilities in order to commercialize new products rapidly in foreign markets. In the past, companies from industrialized countries located manufacturing facilities abroad primarily to benefit from lower wages or to overcome trade barriers. Over time, however, many of those plants have taken on increasingly complex manufacturing tasks that require having an R&D facility nearby in order to ensure the speedy transfer of technology from research to manufacturing. A silicon-wafer plant, for example, has to interact closely with product development engineers during trial runs of a new generation of microchips. The same is true for the manufacture of disk drives and other complex hardware. For that reason, Hewlett-Packard and Texas Instruments both operate laboratories in Singapore, close to manufacturing facilities.

The more complex and varied a manufacturing process is, the more often manufacturing engineers will have to interact with product development engineers. For example, in the case of one of Toshiba's laptop-computer-manufacturing plants, a new model is introduced to the manufacturing line every two weeks. The introduction has to happen seamlessly, without disturbing the production of existing models on the same line. In order to predict and remedy bugs during initial production runs, development engineers and manufacturing engineers meet several times a week. The proximity of Toshiba's laptop-development laboratory to its manufacturing plant greatly facilitates the interaction.

Establishing a New R&D Facility

Whether establishing a home-base-augmenting or a home-base-exploiting facility, companies must use the same three-stage process: selecting the best laboratory leader, determining the optimal size for the new laboratory site, and keeping close watch over the lab during its start-up period in order to ensure that it is merged into the company's existing global R&D network and contributes sufficiently to the company's product portfolio and its economic performance.

SELECTING THE BEST SITE LEADER

Identifying the best leader for a new R&D site is one of the most important decisions a company faces in its quest to establish a successful global R&D network. My research shows that the initial leader of an R&D site has a powerful impact not only on the culture of the site but also on its long-term research agenda and performance. The two types of sites require different types of leaders, and each type of leader confronts a particular set of challenges.

The initial leaders of home-base-augmenting sites should be prominent local scientists so that they will be able to fulfill their primary responsibility: to nurture ties between the new site and the local scientific community. If the site does not succeed in becoming part of the local scientific community quickly, it will not be able to generate new knowledge for the company. In addition to hiring a local scientist, there are a variety of other ways to establish local ties. For example, Toshiba used its memory-chip joint venture with Siemens to develop local ties at its new R&D site in Regensburg, Germany. The venture allowed Toshiba to tap into Siemens's dense network of associations with local universities. In addition, it helped Toshiba develop a better understanding of the compensation packages required to hire first-class German engineering graduates. Finally, it let the company gain useful insights into how to establish effective contract-research relationships with government-funded research institutions in Germany.

> *The best managers of foreign R&D sites are respected scientists or engineers and, at the same time, skilled managers.*

In contrast, the initial leaders of home-base-exploiting sites should be highly regarded managers from within the company—managers who are intimately familiar with the company's culture and systems. Such leaders will be able to fulfill their primary responsibility: to forge close ties between the new lab's engineers and the foreign community's manufacturing and marketing facilities. Then the transfer of knowledge from the company's home base to the R&D site will have the maximum impact on manufacturing and marketing located near that site. When one U.S. pharmaceutical company established a home-base-exploiting site in Great Britain, executives appointed as the initial site leader a manager who had been with the company for several years. He had started his career as a bench scientist first in exploratory research, then in the development of one of the company's blockbuster drugs. He had worked closely with marketing, and he had spent two years as supervisor of manufacturing quality at one of the company's U.S. manufacturing sites. With such a background, he was able to lead the new site effectively.

However, the best candidates for both home-base-augmenting and home-base-exploiting sites share four qualities: they are at once respected scientists or engineers and skilled managers; they are able to integrate the new site into the company's existing R&D network; they have a comprehensive understanding of technology trends; and they are able to overcome formal barriers when they seek access to new ideas in local universities and scientific communities.

Appointing an outstanding scientist or engineer who has no management experience can be disastrous. In one case, a leading U.S. electronics company decided to establish a home-base-augmenting site in the United

Kingdom. The engineer who was appointed as the first site leader was an outstanding researcher but had little management experience outside the company's central laboratory environment. The leader had difficulties marshaling the necessary resources to expand the laboratory beyond its starting size of 14 researchers. Furthermore, he had a tough time mediating between the research laboratory and the company's product development area. Eleven of the 14 researchers had been hired locally and therefore lacked deep ties to the company. They needed a savvy corporate advocate who could understand company politics and could promote their research results within the company. One reason they didn't have such an advocate was that two of the three managers at the company's home base—people who had promoted the establishment of the new R&D lab— had quit about six months after the lab had opened because they disagreed about the company's overall R&D strategy. The third manager had moved to a different department.

In an effort to improve the situation, the company appointed a U.S. engineer as liaison to the U.K. site. He realized that few ideas were flowing from the site to the home base; but he attributed the problem to an inherently slow scientific-discovery process rather than to organizational barriers within the company. After about two years, senior management finally replaced the initial laboratory leader and the U.S. liaison engineer with two managers—one from the United Kingdom and one from the United States. The managers had experience overseeing one of the company's U.S. joint ventures in technology, and they also had good track records as researchers. Finally, under their leadership, the site dramatically increased its impact on the company's product portfolio. In conjunction with the increase in scientific output, the site grew to its projected size of 225 employees and is now highly productive.

In the case of both types of sites, the ideal leader has in-depth knowledge of both the home-base culture and the foreign culture. Consider Sharp's experience. In Japan, fewer corporate scientists have Ph.D.'s than their counterparts in the United Kingdom; instead they have picked up their knowledge and skills on the job. That difference presented a management challenge for Sharp when it established a home-base-augmenting facility in the United Kingdom. In order to cope with that challenge, the company hired a British laboratory leader who had previously worked as a science attaché at the British embassy in Japan. In that position, he had developed a good understanding of the Japanese higher-education system. He was well aware that British and Japanese engineers with different academic degrees might have similar levels of expertise, and, as a result, he could manage them better.

The pioneer who heads a newly established home-base-augmenting or home-base-exploiting site also must have a broad perspective and a deep understanding of technology trends. R&D sites abroad are often particularly good at combining knowledge from different scientific fields into new ideas and products. Because those sites start with a clean slate far from the company's powerful central laboratory, they are less plagued by the "not-invented-here" syndrome. For example, Canon's home-base-augmenting laboratory in the United Kingdom developed an innovative loudspeaker that is now being manufactured in Europe for a worldwide market. Senior researchers at Canon in Japan acknowledge that it would have been much more difficult for a new research team located in Japan to come up with the product. As one Canon manager puts it, "Although the new loudspeaker was partially based on knowledge that existed within Canon already, Canon's research management in Japan was too focused on existing product lines and would probably not have tolerated the pioneering loudspeaker project."

Finally, leaders of new R&D sites need to be aware of the considerable formal barriers they might confront when they seek access to local universities and scientific communities. These barriers are often created by lawmakers who want to protect a nation's intellectual capital. Although foreign companies do indeed absorb local knowledge and transfer it to their home bases—particularly in the case of home-base-augmenting sites—they also create important positive economic effects for the host nation. The laboratory leader of a new R&D site needs to communicate that fact locally in order to reduce existing barriers and prevent the formation of new ones.

DETERMINING THE OPTIMAL SIZE OF THE NEW R&D SITE

My research indicates that the optimal size for a new foreign R&D facility during the start-up phase is usually 30 to 40 employees, and the best size for a site after the ramp-up period is about 235 employees, including support staff. The optimal size of a site depends mainly on a company's track record in international management. Companies that already operate several sites abroad tend to be more successful at establishing larger new sites.

Companies can run into problems if their foreign sites are either too small or too large. If the site is too small, the resulting lack of critical mass produces an environment in which there is little cross-fertilization of ideas among researchers. And a small R&D site generally does not command a sufficient level of respect in the scientific community surrounding the laboratory. As a result, its researchers have a harder time gaining access to informal networks and to scientific meetings that provide opportunities for an exchange of knowledge. In contrast, if the laboratory site is too large, its culture quickly becomes anonymous, researchers become isolated, and the benefits of spreading fixed costs over a larger number of researchers are outweighed by the lack of cross-fertilization of ideas. According to one manager at such a lab, "Once people stopped getting to know one another on an informal basis in the lunchroom of our site, they became afraid of deliberately walking into one another's laboratory rooms to talk about research and to ask questions. Researchers who do not know each other on an informal basis are often hesitant to ask their colleagues for advice: they are afraid to reveal any of their own knowledge gaps. We realized that we had crossed a critical threshold in size. We subsequently scaled back somewhat and made an increased effort to reduce the isolation of individual researchers within the site through communication tools and through rotating researchers among different lab units at the site."

SUPERVISING THE START-UP PERIOD

During the initial growth period of an R&D site, which typically lasts anywhere from one to three years, the culture is formed and the groundwork for the site's future productivity is laid. During that period, senior management in the home country has to be in particularly close contact with the new site. Although it is important that the new laboratory develop its own identity and stake out its fields of expertise, it also has to be closely connected to the company's existing R&D structure. Newly hired scientists must be aware of the resources that exist within the company as a whole, and scientists at home and at other locations must be aware of the opportunities the new site creates for the company as a whole. Particularly during the start-up period, senior R&D managers at the corporate level have to walk a fine line and decide whether to devote the most resources to connecting the new site to the company or to supporting ties between the new site and its local environment.

Managers must integrate a site's research agenda into the company's overall goals.

To integrate a new site into the company as a whole, managers must pay close attention to the site's research agenda and create mechanisms to integrate it into the company's overall strategic goals. Because of the high degree of uncertainty of R&D outcomes, continuous adjustments to research agendas are the rule. What matters most is speed, both in terms of terminating research projects that go nowhere and in terms of pushing projects that bring unexpectedly good results.

The rapid exchange of information is essential to integrating a site into the overall company during the start-up phase. Companies use a number of mechanisms to create a cohesive research community in spite of geographic distance. Hewlett-Packard regularly organizes an in-house science fair at which teams of researchers can present projects and prototypes to one another. Canon has a program that lets researchers from home-base-augmenting sites request a temporary transfer to home-base-exploiting sites. At Xerox, most sites are linked by a sophisticated information system that allows senior R&D managers to determine within minutes the current state of research projects and the number of researchers working on those projects. But nothing can replace face-to-face contact between active researchers. Maintaining a global R&D network requires personal meetings, and therefore many researchers and R&D managers have to spend time visiting not only other R&D sites but also specialized suppliers and local universities affiliated with those sites.

Failing to establish sufficient ties with the company's existing R&D structure during the start-up phase can hamper the success of a new foreign R&D site. For example, in 1986, a large foreign pharmaceutical company established a biotechnology research site in Boston, Massachusetts. In order to recruit outstanding scientists and maintain a high level of creative output, the company's R&D management decided to give the new laboratory considerable leeway in its research agenda and in determining what to do with the results—although the company did reserve the right of first refusal for the commercialization of the lab's inventions. The new site was staffed exclusively with scientists handpicked by a newly hired laboratory leader. A renowned local biochemist, he had been employed for many years by a major U.S. university, where he had carried out contract research for the company. During the

Managing an R&D network is both delicate and complex. It requires constant tinkering—evaluation and reevaluation.

start-up phase, few of the company's veteran scientists were involved in joint research projects with the site's scientists—an arrangement that hindered the transfer of ideas between the new lab and the company's other R&D sites. Although the academic community now recognizes the lab as an important contributor to the field, few of its inventions have been patented by the company, fewer have been targeted for commercialization, and none have reached the commercial stage yet. One senior scientist working in the lab commented that ten years after its creation, the lab had become so much of an "independent animal" that it would take a lot of carefully balanced guidance from the company to instill a stronger sense of commercial orientation without a risk of losing the most creative scientists.

There is no magic formula that senior managers can follow to ensure the success of a foreign R&D site during its start-up phase. Managing an R&D network, particularly in its early stages, is delicate and complex. It requires constant tinkering—evaluation and reevaluation. Senior R&D managers have to decide how much of the research should be initiated by the company and how much by the scientist, determine the appropriate incentive structures and employment contracts, establish policies for the temporary transfer of researchers to the company's other R&D or manufacturing sites, and choose universities from which to hire scientists and engineers.

Flexibility and experimentation during a site's start-up phase can ensure its future productivity. For example, Fujitsu established a software-research laboratory site in San Jose, California, in 1992. The company was seriously thinking of establishing a second site in Boston

but eventually reconsidered. Fujitsu realized that the
effort that had gone into establishing the San Jose site
had been greater than expected. Once the site was up
and running, however, its productive output also had
been higher than expected. Furthermore, Fujitsu found
that its R&D managers had gained an excellent understanding of the R&D community that created advanced
software-development tools. Although initially leaning
toward establishing a second site, the managers were
flexible. They decided to enlarge the existing site
because of its better-than-expected performance as well
as the limited potential benefits of a second site. The
San Jose site has had a major impact on Fujitsu's software development and sales—particularly in Japan but
in the United States, too. Similarly, at Alcatel's first
foreign R&D site in Germany, senior managers were
flexible. After several months, they realized that the
travel-and-communications budget would have to be
increased substantially beyond initial projections in
order to improve the flow of knowledge from the French
home base. For instance, in the case of a telephone
switchboard project, the actual number of business trips
between the two sites was nearly twice as high as originally projected.

Integrating the Global R&D Network

As the number of companies' R&D sites at home and
abroad grows, R&D managers will increasingly face the
challenging task of coordinating the network. That will
require a fundamental shift in the role of senior managers at the central lab. Managers of R&D networks
must be global coordinators, not local administrators.
More than being managers of people and processes, they

must be managers of knowledge. And not all managers that a company has in place will be up to the task.

Consider Matsushita's R&D management. A number of technically competent managers became obsolete at the company once it launched a global approach to R&D. Today managers at Matsushita's central R&D site in Hirakata, Japan, continue to play an important role in the research and development of core processes for manufacturing. But the responsibility of an increasing number of senior managers at the central site is overseeing Matsushita's network of 15 dedicated R&D sites. That responsibility includes setting research agendas, monitoring results, and creating direct ties between sites.

How does the new breed of R&D manager coordinate global knowledge? Look again to Matsushita's central R&D site. First, high-level corporate managers in close cooperation with senior R&D managers develop an overall research agenda and assign different parts of it to individual sites. The process is quite tricky. It requires that the managers in charge have a good understanding of not only the technological capabilities that Matsushita will need to develop in the future but also the stock of technological capabilities already available to it.

Matsushita's central lab organizes two or three yearly off-site meetings devoted to informing R&D scientists and engineers about the entire company's current state of technical knowledge and capabilities. At the same meetings, engineers who have moved from R&D to take over manufacturing and marketing responsibilities inform R&D members about trends in Matsushita's current and potential future markets. Under the guidance of senior project managers, members from R&D, manufacturing, and marketing determine timelines and resource requirements for specific home-base-augmenting and home-base-exploiting projects. One R&D manager notes, "We discuss not only why a specific scientific insight might be interesting for Matsushita but also how we can turn this insight into a product quickly. We usually seek to develop a prototype early. Prototypes are a good basis for a discussion with marketing and manufacturing. Most of our efforts are targeted at delivering the prototype of a slightly better mousetrap early rather than delivering the blueprint of a much better mousetrap late."

To stimulate the exchange of information, R&D managers at Matsushita's central lab create direct links among researchers across different sites. They promote the use of videoconferencing and frequent face-to-face contact to forge those ties. Reducing the instances in which the central lab must act as mediator means that existing knowledge travels more quickly through the company and new ideas percolate more easily. For example, a researcher at a home-base-exploiting site in Singapore can communicate with another researcher at a home-base-exploiting site in Franklin Park, Illinois, about potential new research projects much more readily now that central R&D fosters informal and formal direct links.

Finally, managers at Matsushita's central lab constantly monitor new regional pockets of knowledge as well as the company's expanding network of manufacturing sites to determine whether the company will need additional R&D locations. With 15 major sites around the world, Matsushita has decided that the number of sites is sufficient at this point. But the company is ever vigilant about surveying the landscape and knows that as the landscape changes, its decision could, too.

AS MORE POCKETS OF KNOWLEDGE EMERGE
worldwide and competition in foreign markets mounts,
the imperative to create global R&D networks will grow
all the more pressing. Only those companies that
embrace a global approach to R&D will meet the competitive challenges of the new dynamic. And only those
managers who embrace their fundamentally new role as
global coordinators and managers of knowledge will be
able to tap the full potential of their R&D networks.

Home-Base-Augmenting and Home-Base-Exploiting Sites: Xerox and Eli Lilly

THE PARTICULAR TYPE of foreign R&D site determines the
specific challenges managers will face. Setting up a
home-base-augmenting site—one designed to gather new
knowledge for a company—involves certain skills. And
launching a *home-base-exploiting site*—one established to
help a company efficiently commercialize its R&D in foreign markets—involves others. The cases of Xerox and Eli
Lilly present an instructive contrast.

Xerox established a home-base-augmenting laboratory
in Grenoble, France. Its objective: to tap new knowledge
from the local scientific community and to transfer it back
to its home base. Having already established, in 1986, a
home-base-augmenting site in Cambridge, England, Xerox
realized in 1992 that the research culture in continental
Western Europe was sufficiently different and complementary to Great Britain's to justify another site. Moreover,
understanding the most advanced research in France or
Germany was very difficult from a base in Great Britain

because of language and cultural barriers. One senior R&D manager in the United States notes, "We wanted to learn firsthand what was going on in centers of scientific excellence in Europe. Being present at a center of scientific excellence is like reading poetry in the original language."

It was essential that managers from the highest levels of the company be involved in the decision-making process from the start. Senior scientists met with high-level managers and entered into a long series of discussions. Their first decision: to locate the new laboratory at a center of scientific excellence. Xerox also realized that it had to hire a renowned local scientist as the initial laboratory leader. The leader needed to be able to understand the local scientific community, attract junior scientists with high potential, and target the right university institutes and scholars for joint research projects. Finally, Xerox knew that the laboratory would have an impact on the company's economic performance only if it had the critical mass to become an accepted member of the local scientific community. At the same time, it could not become isolated from the larger Xerox culture.

Xerox considered a number of locations and carefully evaluated such aspects as their scientific excellence and relevance, university liaison programs, licensing programs, and university recruiting programs. The company came up with four potential locations: Paris, Grenoble, Barcelona, and Munich. At that point, Xerox also identified potential laboratory leaders. The company chose Grenoble on the basis of its demonstrated scientific excellence and hired as the initial laboratory leader a highly regarded French scientist with good connections to local universities. Xerox designed a facility for 40 researchers and made plans for further expansion. In order to integrate the new laboratory's scientists into the Xerox community, senior R&D management in Palo Alto, California, allocated a considerable part of the initial laboratory budget to travel to other Xerox sites and started a program for the temporary transfer of newly hired researchers from Grenoble to other R&D sites. At the same time, the Grenoble site set out to integrate itself within the local research community.

In 1989, Eli Lilly considered establishing a home-base-exploiting laboratory in East Asia. The company's objective was to commercialize its R&D more effectively in foreign markets. Until then, Eli Lilly had operated one home-base-augmenting laboratory site abroad and some small sites in industrialized countries for clinical testing and drug approval procedures. But in order to exploit Lilly's R&D capabilities and product portfolio, the company needed a dedicated laboratory site in East Asia. The new site would support efforts to manufacture and market pharmaceuticals by adapting products to local needs. To that end, the management team decided that the new laboratory would have to be located close to relevant markets and existing corporate facilities. It also determined that the initial laboratory leader would have to be an experienced manager from Lilly's home base—a manager with a deep understanding of both the company's local operations and its overall R&D network.

The team considered Singapore as a potential location because of its proximity to a planned Lilly manufacturing site in Malaysia. But ultimately it decided that the new home-base-exploiting laboratory would have the strongest impact on Lilly's sales if it was located in Kōbe, Japan. By establishing a site in the Kōbe-Osaka region—the second-largest regional market in Japan and one that offered educational institutions with high-quality scientists—Lilly would send a signal to the medical community there that the company was committed to the needs of the Japanese market. Kōbe had another advantage: Lilly's corporate headquarters for Japan were located there, and the company was already running some of its drug approval operations for the Japanese market out of Kōbe. The city therefore was the logical choice.

The team assigned an experienced Lilly researcher and manager to be the initial leader of the new site. Because he knew the company inside and out—from central research and development to international marketing—the team reasoned that he would be able to bring the new laboratory up to speed quickly by drawing on resources from various divisions within Lilly. In order to integrate the new site into the over-all company, some researchers from other Lilly R&D sites received temporary transfers of up to two years to Kōbe, and some locally hired researchers were temporarily transferred to other Lilly sites. It took about 30 months to activate fully the Kōbe operation—a relatively short period. Today the site is very productive in transferring knowledge from Lilly's home base to Kōbe and in commercializing that knowledge throughout Japan and Asia.

Notes

1. In a systematic effort to analyze the relationship of global strategy and R&D investments in technologically intensive industries, I have been collecting detailed data on all dedicated laboratory sites operated by 32 leading multinational companies. The sample consists of 10 U.S., 12 Japanese, and 10 European companies. Thirteen of the companies are in the pharmaceutical industry, and 19 are

in the electronics industry. Data collection includes archival research, a detailed questionnaire, and in-depth interviews with several senior R&D managers in each company. Overall, these companies operate 238 dedicated R&D sites, 156 of them abroad. About 60% of the laboratory sites abroad were established after 1984. I have used this sample, which is the most complete of its kind, as a basis for a number of quantitative and qualitative investigations into global strategy, competitive interaction, and R&D management.

2. My research on global R&D strategies builds on earlier research on the competitiveness of nations and on research on foreign direct investment, including Michael E. Porter, *The Competitive Advantage of Nations* (New York: The Free Press, 1990), and Thomas J. Wesson, "An Alternative Motivation for Foreign Direct Investment" (Ph.D. dissertation, Harvard University, 1993). My research also builds on an existing body of knowledge about the management of multinational companies. See, for example, Christopher A. Bartlett and Sumantra Ghoshal, *Managing Across Borders* (New York: The Free Press, 1989).

Originally published in March–April 1997
Reprint 97206

Defining Next-Generation Products

An Inside Look

BEHNAM TABRIZI AND RICK WALLEIGH

Executive Summary

THE CONTINUED SUCCESS of technology-based companies depends on their proficiency in creating next-generation products and their derivatives. So getting such products out the door on schedule must be routine for such companies, right?

Not quite. The authors recently engaged in a detailed study—in which they had access to sensitive internal information and to candid interviews with people at every level—of 28 next-generation product-development projects in 14 leading high-tech companies. They found that most of the companies were unable to complete such projects on schedule. And the companies also had difficulty developing the derivative products needed to fill the gaps in the market that their next-generation products would create.

The problem in every case, the authors discovered, was rooted in the product definition phase. And not coincidentally, the successful companies in the study had all learned how to handle the technical and marketplace uncertainties in their product definition processes. The authors have discerned from the actions of those companies a set of best practices that can measurably improve the definition phase of any company's product-development process. They have grouped the techniques into three categories and carefully lay out the steps that companies need to take as they work through each stage.

The best practices revealed here are not a magic formula for rapid, successful new-product definition. But they can help companies capture new markets without major delays. And that is good news for any manager facing the uncertainty that goes with developing products for a global marketplace.

THE CREATION OF NEXT-GENERATION products and their derivatives would seem to be the routine work of technology-based companies. Their continued business success, after all, depends on it.

Yet in a detailed study of 28 next-generation product-development projects at 14 leading high-tech companies, we found that most of the companies were unable to complete such projects on schedule. Furthermore, they had difficulty developing the derivative products needed to fill the gaps in the market that their next-generation products would create. Of the companies we studied—which ranged in size from $500 million to more than $10 billion in annual sales—the next-

generation products of only four successfully met their
developers' expectations about schedule, specification,
and market share. The next-generation products of five
companies appeared successful to outside observers
but did not meet internal goals or market-share aspira-
tions. The new products of the remaining five companies
were wholly unsuccessful. We also found that in every
case where delays and difficulties occurred, they origi-
nated in the definition phase of the company's product-
development process—that is, before the organization
had committed itself to a specific product design.

Next-generation products—also known as platform
products because they are expected to inspire and support a whole new line of derivative products—require a
major commitment of resources. Like Volvo's 850, which
introduced five-cylinder, front-wheel-drive cars to the
company's line, and Boeing's 777, which substantially
improved on the range and efficiency of its 737 line of
aircraft, a platform product incorporates significant
improvements in performance and cost over the preced-
ing generation's product. It addresses the needs of future
customers while providing a path for current customers
to migrate from the older product.[1]

A panel of consulting and academic experts picked
the 14 companies that we examined. Guarantees of
anonymity helped ensure our access to the companies'
most sensitive internal information and to candid interviews with people at every level. We had access, for
instance, to business and product-definition plans, team
meeting minutes, information about product development processes, and postproject assessments.

What sets the adept minority of these companies
apart from the rest? The nine companies that failed to
meet their own expectations did so for many different

reasons, but the successful companies were all successful for the same reasons. Thus we have been able to
discern from the latter group's actions a set of best practices that can measurably improve the definition
phase—or "fuzzy front end"—of any company's product-
development process.

We have not discovered a magic formula for rapid,
successful new-product definition. Because new-
platform products are developed to serve the future
needs of customers, companies are at high risk when
they work with new, unproved technologies or architectures. Furthermore, given the volatile nature of their
industries, high-tech companies have difficulty predict-
ing how their markets will move over time. Uncertainty
promotes bickering among groups within the organization and indecision by managers—and leads to chaos in
product development.

The successful companies we studied had all learned
to deal with the technical and marketplace uncertainties.
That is, they had learned how to overcome the chaos in
their product definition processes. And while they all
used roughly the same techniques, they had derived
those techniques quite independently. We have grouped
the techniques into three categories: *product strategy,
project organization*, and *execution during the definition
stage*.[2] These categories do not encompass everything a
company needs to do as it defines a platform product.
Rather, they provide a useful way to cluster and think
about the best practices we have identified.

Product Strategy

We have bunched three best practices for product development under the rubric of product strategy. The first is

to create a clear map of the company's product stream for the next two years and to use it to manage all aspects of the company's development activities. The second is to generate a seamless product strategy—that is, one that leaves no holes for competitors to exploit. The third is to collect, interpret, and assimilate good information about the market.

Creating and using a map of the company's new-product stream. Most companies use some sort of strategic-planning process to clarify their vision and then map the product development activity required to realize it. The maps define a stream of products, including platform products and their derivatives, that the company is committed to developing over the next two years. The main value of the maps lies not in any certainty about the future that they might imply. Indeed, the maps are revised frequently. Rather, they help force the company to make decisions about new projects for platform products amid the uncertainty that characterizes rapidly shifting markets and evolving technologies.

All the companies in our study had product maps. The differences between the successes and the failures lay in how they used the maps as management tools.

The organizational process used to build commitment among senior managers while they create a product map is critical. One successful company draws its product maps at senior management retreats in order to promote cohesion, commitment, and clarity throughout the organization regarding the sequence and timing of new products. In that setting, all managers, regardless of their function, begin to grasp the significance of the new products for the organization—how and when they will have an impact on marketing, distribution, technology, and service. Mapping also illuminates major resource decisions affecting the execution of the new-platform product. The process of creating a map forces senior management to face up to tough choices—whether to increase funding for a product line in order to become a market leader, when and where to dampen support for maturing products, and how to tackle the inevitable trade-offs between promising individual projects and overall strategic direction.

Once drawn, maps are not set in concrete. The volatility of technology and technology markets permits no such luxury. The company referred to above holds its senior management retreats every six months and redraws the map at each retreat. Furthermore, the senior management team revisits and updates its plans bimonthly between retreats so that the document is always current.

In the underperforming companies we studied, the product maps were two-dimensional charts lacking in substance. They gave senior managers the false sense that future plans were in place. In fact, however, little if any thought had been given to budgets, organizational issues, or technology requirements. Consequently, the maps had no value as planning tools, and every step of the product definition process generated its own crisis.

It is in the nature of platform products to expose greater markets than they can cover.

The senior members of one troubled platform-project team we examined spent two years revising their definition of the product while marketing and manufacturing maintained their own separate definitions. When asked later about their overarching strategy for the product, the senior members claimed that they had been too busy to address such broad issues earlier. The company's mapping process was a hollow exercise that did not force anyone to anticipate such questions. Not surprisingly, the entire organization remained confused about the product and its market positioning right up to the time of its introduction.

In contrast, another company we examined demonstrated the value of the mapping process when it had to choose among 50 proposed projects. It used its map to define key priorities, reach timely decisions, and define the new-platform products. Furthermore, because of the efficiency introduced by the mapping process, the company could downsize its development organization and use the savings to fund several marketing initiatives and a strategically critical acquisition. Thus the process of mapping not only yields better results in final products but also eliminates wasted effort that distracts an organization from more important work. In the best companies, the product maps and the processes used to create them are the centerpiece of the entire product-development process.

Building a product strategy without holes. It is in the nature of platform products to expose greater markets than they themselves cover. Successful companies make plans to fill those holes with derivative products even while they are defining the platform product that will create the gaps. Companies that don't make such plans hand rich opportunities to their competitors, who may even dislodge them from the very markets that they have created. (See the exhibit "Platform Products and the Gaps They Create.")

The successful companies we studied made sure they understood who was buying their current products and why, so that they could make informed judgments about the gaps in the market that their new products would create. Then they could decide how to protect those gaps—and their existing markets—from new entrants. Several companies made their existing offerings more attractive by discounting, adding new features, or running promotional pricing campaigns. They also quickly offered scaled-down versions of their new products in order to hold on to the low end of the market they had just created. (See "Dreams and Nightmares" at the end of this article.)

Platform Products and the Gaps They Create

New-platform products create marketplace gaps that competitors can exploit. Companies should plan to fill the gaps with derivative products even while they are defining the new platform itself.

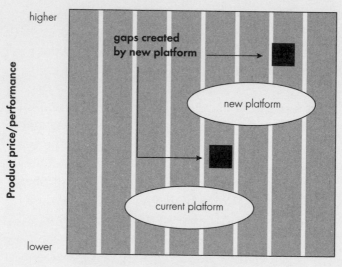

Market segments

Getting good market information. Effective product definition demands good market information. The companies we found to be successful at introducing new-platform products maintained continual, open-ended conversations with their customers. In particular, those companies made an effort to identify the pioneers and risk takers among their customers—the people most likely to push the existing products to their performance limits. Product team leaders maintained an ongoing dialogue with those leading-edge customers, sharing information about technical trends, predictions made in the trade press, and updates on progress and possible applications of new products. Team leaders asked pointed questions: What would help your company accomplish its objectives? What new features would be useful? What are your cost constraints? What features could be eliminated to meet your needs at the right cost?

But successful companies talked to more than just current customers. They developed processes to query prospective customers, indirect sales channels such as retailers and wholesalers, clients of current customers, and even former customers. Those companies were determined to develop assessments of the potential success of new products that would be untainted by the bias of their largest and most supportive customers. They wanted to know, in other words, what the market expected.

Project Organization

The organizational characteristics of a company's platform-product-development process are crucial to its timely and effective execution. Our study uncovered three best practices relating to project organization. The first is the willingness to turn the development of new-platform products over to business units created solely for that purpose. The second is knowing how to choose the optimum number of members—with the right mix of skills—for the product definition team over the course of the product development process. And the third is the ability to match other product-development resources—such as the shifting workloads of engineers and marketers—to the cyclical demands of the process.

Creating new business units for new markets.
When a company intends its new-platform product to make a quantum leap in performance in comparison with the current product, it will probably need to design a completely new product system and architecture. Moreover, the new product is likely to be addressed more to new customers than to users of the current product. With that in mind, the successful companies in our study sometimes created new business units to develop the new-platform product. They found that internal cultures and processes honed to support one kind of product were ill-suited to the creation and support of a significantly different one. Managers told us that in such situations product development would fare better in a newly created division.

One company, for instance, assigned seasoned talent from three separate product groups to a new division with the sole objective of creating a new family of products. Another corporation used the facilities of a recently acquired company to house a new project team thousands of miles (and several time zones) away from corporate headquarters. The team itself consisted largely of new hires—people with strong engineering backgrounds, a desire for visible results, and little patience for bureaucratic procedures.

In both cases, the companies encouraged the newly formed groups to behave entrepreneurially; that is, to create their own three-year business plans and to begin generating revenue as quickly as possible by cobbling together products that would get them into the market— all the while working on the new-platform design. Both companies supported the new units through the loan of corporate resources from marketing, distribution, and sales—resources that would help the new enterprise gain an early foothold in the market it was targeting.

Staffing the platform-product-definition team.

Assigning too many people to platform-product-defini-tion teams too early can delay the definition process and blunt the results. One company assigned more than 30 engineers to the formative phase of a development pro-ject, causing a senior manager to complain that "we had too many engineers spinning their wheels while the defi-nition kept changing." Now the company begins new projects with no more than five engineers and one mar-ket strategist to define the overall framework. It adds new people to work on the details after the small team has fixed the initial specifications.

In addition to needing the right number of employ-ees, an effective platform-product-definition team requires people with the right mix of skills and experi-ence. Senior marketing strategists with a grasp of tech-nology and a feel for the direction of markets and key competitors are best equipped to define new opportuni-ties. Their senior technical counterparts can articulate the possible technological obstacles, cost and time con-straints, and risks. Their seniority and experience gives both functional types the credibility and authority needed to make decisions that cannot easily be overturned and muffles costly second-guessing by others on the team or in management.

The extensive experience these senior marketing and technical staff have acquired should give them a broader perspective than others on the team. Thus they should emerge as influential leaders during all stages of the product development process, tempering the tendency of less-experienced engineers to tweak and fiddle with a design long after it should have been set and discouraging marketers from summarily discounting technical hurdles in a rush to get the product out.

We found that product definition was most successful when initial specifications preceded the final selection of the product development team. We also found that products emerged faster and made more of an impact on the market when product teams included the company's most knowledgeable engineers and marketing strategists from the outset. And we noted that when product development teams were thus staffed, a company's ability to follow through with derivative products, follow-on applications, and ongoing product enhancements was also much greater.

Matching resources during new-platform development. All 14 companies we studied used cross-functional product-development teams, but the successful companies effectively addressed a problem inherent in using such teams. We call the problem *cycle mismatch*. Early in the product development process—in the product definition stage—a team's marketing professionals are busy writing preliminary business plans and, with input from the engineers, determining the market's requirements. The engineers have a lighter load at this stage, but their workload increases as the product's architecture and specifications are developed. Then,

The successful companies released products frequently to fill gaps around new platforms.

during the product development stage, the bulk of the work falls on the engineers. The marketers are much less busy—their role is to watch customers and competitors for shifts in the marketplace. Later, during the product launch stage, the burden on the engineers begins to ease while the work of the marketing people grows as they prepare to promote, deliver, and support the new product. (See the exhibit "Cyclical Workload Mismatch.")

As the relative burden on engineers and marketing professionals reverses, the company may lose the opportunity to begin work on derivative products and new-product enhancements. Such missed opportunities happen because engineers must wait for the now busy

Cyclical Workload Mismatch

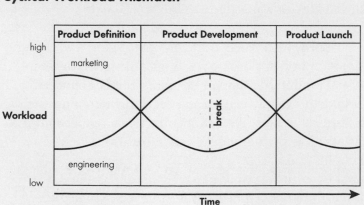

marketing managers to finish the new-platform launch before those managers can help define other new products.

To correct this imbalance, the successful project teams we studied took a scheduled break—which was shown on the companies' product-stream maps— midway through development of the new-platform product. During this brief pause, the team—marketing professionals included—sought to identify markets that would be affected by the new product, to initiate the development of derivatives to fill potentially vulnerable areas, and to assign key engineering and marketing people to the development task.

The companies that took this approach lost no momentum between the launch of their new-platform products and the execution of a seamless market-penetration strategy. As marketers became preoccupied in the later stages of product development, engineers already had the specifications they needed to continue the technical progress on derivative products—and on adding to or enhancing the new-platform product's features. The successful companies all used this approach to create entire families of products by filling the gaps around the new platforms. Thus they created barriers to encroachment on their expanded markets.

Scheduling a pause part way into the product development process does not by itself ensure the development and introduction of derivative and enhanced products. To fully correct the cycle mismatch during the definition of new-platform products, companies need to be sure that four other elements are also in place:

- discipline, which requires the company to establish explicit milestones for a derivative-product-development plan when it is mapping its product stream;

- incentives that reward the members of the marketing and engineering team for success in filling gaps in the marketplace, not just in meeting new-product requirements;

- alignment, which means that senior managers' incentives must be tied to their effectiveness in directing attention to planning for derivative products during the development process; and

- resources ensuring the availability of sufficient key members of the product development team to work on derivative products and platform product enhancements.

The companies successful at filling the gaps around new platforms tended to release new or upgraded products frequently. This rapid-fire approach to product releases forced those organizations to stay abreast of new technology and to look at product development as a continual process. The frequent release of products also helped those companies appeal to many market segments with customized offerings. Necessarily, the companies considered the issues of modularity and scale when they developed a platform product so that they could develop and release derivatives quickly.

Execution During Definition

By *execution during definition*, we refer not to how the best-practice companies actually defined their new-platform products, but to how they tried to ensure that the definition process took place effectively and on schedule. We include three best practices under this third and final rubric.

TRACKING PROGRESS AND
SUSTAINING URGENCY

The root causes of most of the delays we observed during product definition were managerial in nature: the lack of a process to monitor elapsed time and insufficient management attention to the routine aspects of the definition process. Only a few of the 14 organizations maintained a disciplined process for measuring adherence to schedule and the effectiveness of the definition in the earliest stages of a new-platform project. More often, until very late in the product development process, only crises got management's attention. As a result, product launches were late, unfocused, and unsupported by contingency plans or additional resources.

One of the successful companies, however, starts an internal clock as soon as the first meeting about the new-platform product takes place. Thereafter, the company tracks not just time elapsed but also the cost in time of the personnel involved. Doing so establishes and helps maintain a sense of urgency among product-development team members.

Another tool used by managers in the successful companies is a so-called product-priority document. This is nothing more than the traditional product-requirements document, but with required features organized into categories from the customer's point of view. The three categories are "must have," "should have," and "nice to have." Creating the product-priority document forces teams to analyze various trade-offs in detailed discussions with customers. "If we add this feature," the team will ask a customer, "our cost will grow by x dollars and our development schedule will be slowed by y months. Are you willing to pay more and wait longer?"

The product-priority document links the product introduction to the company's overall business strategy and keeps product developers focused on the features that customers want in the order in which they want them. It holds the team to firm deadlines and clear agreements about trade-offs. This approach encourages but at the same time disciplines the "what if" discussions that can delay new-platform development.

The product-priority document intensifies the focus on the new product across functional and managerial lines. And it sets the pace for the product's introduction by establishing a prior-ity of features. If competitive conditions change and it becomes important to enter the market sooner than origi-nally planned, the important but lower-priority features can be held for inclusion in the next set of products.

Product team members met early with senior management to decide how long the team would be allowed to "play in the sand."

The best-practice companies employ a third technique to sustain urgency. Senior members of the product team—both engineers and marketers—meet early in the process with senior management and decide how long the team will be allowed to "play in the sand"—that is, how much time it will have to create a definition of the new product. And senior managers continue to meet weekly with these senior team members to check their progress against the schedule and to review the team's resource needs.

In one company, after a new-platform definition and milestones had emerged, the project entered what the company called the *commitment gate*—a mechanism for freezing the platform definition and specifications. At that point, team members and senior managers articulated and understood all requirements. The development team committed to a delivery date, and everyone involved knew that only dramatic changes in technology, markets, or corporate resources could reopen those decisions.

The companies that used a commitment-gate model continued to gather information from customers and others right through the product launch. They did not ignore the market as it changed around them, but they were in a position to know which changes could wait to be accommodated later, with derivative products. Most companies in our study lacked a commitment gate. Various parts of the organizations were continually changing product definitions, in some cases until just weeks before the launch date—thus inducing delay after delay.

DEVELOPING EARLY PROTOTYPES

The successful companies we studied moved quickly to develop prototypes of the key subsystems of their new product—and then of the entire system. Because they skipped the usual proof-of-concept stage, their prototypes often weren't perfect, requiring software fixes, rewiring, and even minor redesign. But the delays thus incurred were small and cheap relative to the advantages gained.

Early prototypes excited and energized the product team in ways that less palpable representations of the new product or its subsystems could not. With prototypes available, team members' discussions were more focused and concrete, and decisions were made more quickly.

Successful organizations also found that customers are willing editors and critics. When given a working model or system component for comment, they talked about the features they liked, desirable attributes they missed, and a variety of interface and ergonomic issues (screens and switches, for example). The feedback provided by customers at this stage helped product developers reconcile desired features with the constraints of time and cost.

Successful companies also stayed in touch with customers, even as late as the week the new products were shipped, to gather information about potential needs and early changes that could be incorporated into future versions of the product. Those companies have created processes that allow them to maintain close relationships with their customers throughout the product's introduction and its refinement. The customer dialogue doesn't delay product development. Rather, it provides a continuous stream of market information that helps shape derivatives and revisions.

USING DEVELOPMENT PARTNERSHIPS

A few of the companies we studied elected to form partnerships with key suppliers to develop new-platform products. In some cases, the codeveloper brought a set of skills and experiences that complemented the strengths of the marketing partner; in others, the partner offered financial resources or useful technology. In several cases, however, major differences in style, priorities, and motivation created costly delays and revisions.

Most of the issues that threatened to derail the codevelopment ventures were resolved at the working level, not by contract amendments or litigation. Project leaders found that when companies shared people and technology, the differences narrowed and momentum was regained. That was particularly true when cooperating companies shared engineers—by swapping them between companies, for instance, or by having engineers from both companies work together at a single site. Any issues in one organization—specifications, standards, or milestones, for instance—quickly became matters of common concern.

Engineers working closely together on site developed a common language and a common set of tools and methodologies to use in developing the new product. One successful codeveloper reported that exchanges of engineers allowed each company to monitor the progress of the entire project with greater certainty. Using a common methodology, engineers from both companies were able to check the alignment of their individual efforts frequently and spot potential problems early. Their growing comfort with the codevelopment process enabled both partners to proceed confidently with their respective portions of the project. Like allied armies, codeveloping partners can surmount differences in style and culture when they are working together in pursuit of shared goals.

Beyond New-Platform Development

When a company treats the successful launch of a new-platform product as an isolated event rather than part of an ongoing process, competitors with imitative products can quickly take possession of the market gap the new platform creates. The companies we studied reported concern and frustration as they watched other companies exploit opportunities they had overlooked. So it is important to note once again that overall market success depends not only on a company's development of new-platform products but also on its ability to create the derivative products that can insulate its share of the market from competitors' incursions. The process entailed in defining derivative products, however, is markedly different from the process for defining platform products.

While the uncertainty surrounding new-platform-product definition requires a small, focused working group, a derivatives team needs to be fully staffed at the outset to develop a comprehensive plan for reaching the target markets rapidly. And good process management necessitates the short-term tracking of goals for derivatives teams, with an emphasis on measuring their progress toward key milestones. (See the chart "New-Product-Definition Processes.")

Among the successful companies we studied, the effective derivatives teams launched their work with an off-site meeting to reach consensus on the requirements, detailed supporting plans, and timetable. Scheduling was

New-Product-Definition Processes

	Platform products	Derivative products
Uncertainty	High	Low
Definition of specifications	Specifications evolve over time before final definition	Specifications are completed within a few days
Initial staffing of team	Staffed with only key employees	Fully staffed with all employees involved in product development
Milestones	Early: Long intervals between milestones	Short intervals between well-defined milestones
	Later: Short intervals	

especially critical, and key milestones were set at short intervals for easy monitoring. Action plans contained crisp, clear goals, and as the process proceeded, teams recognized individual members for meeting interim milestones and thus keeping the project on track.

A communications-networking company in our study deployed a separate team for derivative development while the new-platform-product project was still under way. The two-track process enabled the platform-product-definition team to distinguish genuine technical obstacles in its path (the "showstoppers") from difficulties the derivatives team could address in periodic upgrades (the "fixies"). This ability allowed the platform development team to retain its urgency.

As POSTREENGINEERED COMPANIES look for ways to grow their businesses after a long campaign to reduce their costs, the best practices of successful product developers can help them capture new markets without major delays. Instead of leaving gaps for competitors to exploit, the successful companies we examined have learned how to define and develop new products in order to maximize their market penetration. Their lessons can be instructive for any manager facing the uncertainty that goes with developing products for a fast-paced global marketplace.

Dreams and Nightmares

INTEL CORPORATION IS a master at filling in the holes it creates by introducing new-platform products. It intro-

duced the Pentium microprocessor to the personal computer market at 60 and 66 MHz clock speeds in March
1993; over time, it released successively faster versions
that recently reached beyond 200 MHz. Each release
involved a price cut that was made possible by cost
reductions. The company also brought out compact versions of the chip for the laptop and notebook markets.
Thus Intel quickly filled all the performance, price, and
application gaps caused by the Pentium and so pre-
empted the competition—every marketer's dream. Similarly, when the company introduced its new-platform Pentium Pro microprocessor, it rapidly filled the market niches
created by that chip. In addition, the new microprocessor
worked with software applications designed for previous
Pentium chips, thus providing a migration path to the new
product for existing customers. And in 1997, the company plugged the gap in the multimedia market by introducing what it called *MMX technology.* The technology
allowed the company's microprocessors, including the
Pentium, to operate effectively with audio, video, games,
and graphics.

Orion Computer (a composite fiction), on the other
hand, experienced a nightmare. Orion, a worldwide
leader in engineering workstations, introduced a feature-
laden model for the networked-engineering-design market
seven months behind schedule. The result of a year's
intensive, often chaotic planning followed by two years'
design and development, the next-generation product
boasted an advanced central-processing unit, exclusive
graphics capability, and even flexible internal-networking
circuitry. But the chaotic development process not only
had created costly delays but also had depressed
morale on the development team to the point that several
key employees left the company. Then, after a couple of

months of successful sales, Orion saw its new market undermined by a competitor's product that offered fewer features and functions than its own but at a much lower price. Orion had nothing to counter the newcomer with and thus surrendered sales and share in the market that its own platform product had created.

Notes

1. The definition of platform product is taken from Kim B. Clark and Steven C. Wheelwright, *Managing New Product and Process Development* (New York: The Free Press, 1993).

2. The authors thank Steven C. Wheelwright, M.B.A. Class of 1949 Professor of Business Administration at the Harvard Business School, for suggesting these three categories.

Originally published in November–December 1997
Reprint 97610

About the Contributors

W. BRIAN ARTHUR is Citibank Professor at the Santa Fe
Institute and PricewaterhouseCoopers Fellow. From 1983 to
1996 he was Dean and Virginia Morrison Professor of Economics and Population Studies at Stanford University. His
main interests are the economics of high technology; the new
economy and how business evolves in an era of high technology; cognition in the economy; and financial markets. Professor Arthur's work on increasing returns won him a Guggen-
heim Fellowship in 1987 and the Schumpeter Prize in
Economics in 1990. Currently, he is also a consultant to Citi-
group, McKinsey & Company, and PricewaterhouseCoopers,
among others.

HENRY W. CHESBROUGH is an assistant professor of business administration, with a joint appointment in the technology and operations management and entrepreneurial management areas, at the Harvard Business School. He has
consulted with leading personal computer hardware, software, and information-service companies in both the United
States and Japan on issues of technology management and
business strategy. Prior to embarking on an academic career,
he spent ten years in various product planning and strategic
marketing positions in Silicon Valley companies.

Following the sale of his company, Vermeer Technologies, to
Microsoft in 1996, **CHARLES H. FERGUSON** has returned to

writing, investing, and academic research. From 1996 to 1997 he held visiting scholar appointments at MIT and the University of California, Berkeley. He is currently completing a book to be published by Random House in the fall of 1999. Dr. Ferguson holds a B.A. in Mathematics from the University of California, Berkeley, and a Ph.D. in Political Science from MIT.

MARCO IANSITI is a professor in technology and operations management at the Harvard Business School. His research focuses on the management of technology and product development. He has worked as a consultant to several major *Fortune* 500 companies and he is an advisor and board member in several leading organizations. His work has appeared in a variety of journals, including the *Harvard Business Review, California Management Review, Research Policy, Industrial and Corporate Change, Production and Operations Management,* and *IEEE Transactions on Engineering Management.* He is the author of *Technology Integration: Making Critical Choices in a Dynamic World* (HBS Press, 1997).

WALTER KUEMMERLE is an assistant professor of business administration and Class of 1961 Fellow at the Harvard Business School, with a joint appointment in the technology and operations management and the entrepreneurial management areas. His research and teaching interests fall within the domain of knowledge and capital management in a global economy, specifically in foreign direct investment, venture capital, and technology strategy of multinational corporations. Professor Kuemmerle's research has appeared in academic journals, the *Harvard Business Review,* and as chapters in several books.

CHARLES R. MORRIS is a former partner at Devonshire Partners, a Cambridge, Massachusetts, technology consulting and financial advisory firm. He is the coauthor, with Charles

H. Ferguson, of *Computer Wars: How the West Can Win in a Post–IBM World.*

GARY P. PISANO is a professor in the technology and operations management area at the Harvard Business School. He has recently completed a multiyear research project on the management of process development and technology transfer in the pharmaceutical and biotechnology industries. His current research examines process innovation and improvement strategies in health care. Professor Pisano is the author of *The Development Factory* (HBS Press, 1996), several articles in academic journals, a casebook with Robert Hayes and David Upton entitled *Strategic Operations: Competing Through Capabilities,* and numerous case studies on product development and manufacturing strategies at such companies as BMW, Eli Lilly, and ITT Automotive.

BEHNAM TABRIZI is a consulting professor of high-tech management at Stanford University. He consults with leading high-tech companies on strategy, product development, and market acceptance (time-to-profit). Professor Tabrizi is recognized as teaching the first Web-based course in the world. He has won teaching awards from his department and the Stanford School of Engineering. His current research is on highly adaptable organizations and organizational transformation through rapid product development and strategic acquisition.

DAVID J. TEECE is the Mitsubishi Bank Professor at the Haas School of Business, director of the Institute of Management, Innovation, and Organization, and director of the Center for Research in Management at the University of California, Berkeley. His interests lie in industrial organization and the economics of technological change. Professor Teece is the coauthor of more than 100 articles and publications, including *The Competitive Challenge* and, with Richard P. Rumelt and Dan E. Schendel, the coeditor of *Fundamental Issues in Strategy* (HBS Press, 1994).

RICK WALLEIGH is a management consulting partner with Ernst & Young LLP in San Jose, California, where he specializes in assisting high-technology companies to become global competitors. His consulting projects focus on improving company operations, including new product development, order management, and manufacturing and global supply chain management. Prior to his consulting career, Mr. Walleigh held several management positions at Hewlett-Packard Corporation. He is the author of several articles in the *Harvard Business Review, Industrial Engineering,* and the *Journal of Business Strategy,* among others.

JONATHAN WEST is an assistant professor at the Harvard Business School. His research on learning in technology development and the acquisition of organizational capabilities in diverse national contexts has appeared in many scholarly journals and as several book chapters. Professor West is currently researching the technology-development strategies of leading semiconductor firms in Europe, Korea, and Taiwan. He is also studying the sources and impact of biotechnological change in global agribusiness. Professor West holds doctoral and master's degrees from Harvard University and has served as consultant to corporations and government agencies around the world.

STEVEN C. WHEELWRIGHT is the Edsel Bryant Ford Professor of Business Administration at the Harvard Business School, where he also serves as a senior associate dean and MBA program chair. In his research, Dr. Wheelwright examines product and process development and their connection to competitive advantage and operations excellence. He has coauthored several works with Harvard Business School colleague Kim Clark, most recently, *Leading Product Development: The Senior Manager's Guide to Creating and Shaping the Enterprise.* Dr. Wheelwright is also the author or coauthor of more than ten other books, as well as numerous articles.

Index

ACE. *See* MIPS Technologies, Advanced Computing Environment

Acuvue contact lens (Johnson & Johnson), 87–89

Adobe, 123
Acrobat, 145
PostScript, 124, 132
PostScript for Fax, 145

Advanced Micro Devices (AMD), 15, 18, 122, 128, 133

airline industry, 164

Alcatel, 190

alignment, and platform product teams, 213

alliances. *See also* virtual organization
architectural competition and, 137–138
organizational strategy and, 34–35
technological ecologies and, 161–162
in U.S. semiconductor industry, 18

AMD. *See* Advanced Micro Devices

Amdahl, 125

America Online, 160, 163

Ameritech, 51–53

antitrust regulation, 168–170

Apple Computer, 41, 122, 130, 136, 142, 151, 161
Apple II, 143
Lisa, 142
Macintosh operating system, 130, 136, 142, 151, 161

Applicon, 130

architectural competition, 117–145
general- *vs.* special-purpose systems and, 130
graphical user interfaces (GUIs) and, 141–142
IBM PC and, 40–43, 129
implementation and, 128–129
low-end *vs.* high-end systems and, 130–131
management of, 135–139

architectural competition (*continued*)
  nonproprietary systems architectures and, 124
  open systems and, 40–43, 120–124, 129–130
  page- and image-description standards and, 144–145
  phases to, 131–135
  point product vendors and, 127
  principles of, 128–135
  Silicon Valley Model and, 135–139
  video games and, 143–144
AT&T, 3, 4, 8, 13, 15, 93, 122
  Bell Laboratories, 9, 13, 179
Autodesk, 130
automobile industry, 115–116
autonomous innovation, 35–38

biotechnology process development, 82
Boeing 777, 201
Borland, 119, 122
Bristol-Myers Squibb, 172
Bull (computer company), 93, 118
BusinessLand, 42

cannibalization, 139
Canon, 172, 179, 184–185, 187
CCITT fax standard, 124
Chandler, Alfred, 49
Chips and Technologies, 119

commitment gate model, 215–216
commitment phase in architectural competition, 131–132
communication. *See also* coordination
  informal channels of, and process development, 82–86
  leaders of foreign R&D sites and, 185
  organizational learning and, 107–110
Compaq, 43, 44, 119–120, 126, 131, 139
competitive advantage. *See also* increasing returns
  architectural control and, 120, 128–135
  changing nature of competition and, 64–68, 71–72
  increasing returns as mechanisms of, 147–148, 149
  process development and, 57–59
  technology integration and, 5–6
  in traditional *vs.* knowledge-based industries, 148–149, 150–151
complexity
  system focus and, 98–99, 115–116
  technology integration and, 24

CompuServe, 163
computer industry
    patterns of success and fail-
        ure in, 118–120
    segmentation in, 6–7
ComputerLand, 41, 42
Conner Peripherals, 122
convenience, and product
    domination, 169
coordination. *See also* commu-
    nication
    autonomous *vs.* systemic
        innovation and, 35–38
    as challenge for virtual orga-
        nization, 34
    global R&D networks and,
        190–193
    industry standards and,
        38–40
    platform product codevel-
        opment and, 217–218
corporate strategy
    global R&D networks and,
        171, 172–173
    platform products and,
        203–205
costs
    of manufacturing,
        72–79
    up-front, and increasing
        returns, 153
cultural awareness, and foreign
    site leadership, 184
customers
    acceptance by, and process
        development, 63

platform product develop-
    ment and, 207, 217
product-use skills and, 154
Cutler, Dave, 134
cycle mismatch, 210–213
Cypress Semiconductor,
    119
Cyrix, 18, 122, 133

Daisy (computer company),
    130
Data General, 118
DEC, 18, 33, 44, 118
    VMS operating system,
        134–135
derivative products, and plat-
    form product definition,
        205–206, 212, 213,
        218–220
diffusion phase in architectural
    competition, 132
diminishing returns. *See also*
    increasing returns
    Alfred Marshall's view of,
        150–151
    shift to increasing returns,
        148–149
    traditional industries and,
        149, 150–151
discipline, and platform prod-
    uct teams, 212
DOS, 127, 139, 142
    IBM organizational strategy
        and, 40, 43
    increasing returns and,
        151–152, 154, 161, 169

dynamic random-access memory (DRAM) chips
  process-development performance comparisons and, 14–17
  technology required for design of, 3–4

Electronic Arts, 143
Eli Lilly, 26, 193, 195–196
EPA. *See* U.S. Environmental Protection Agency
execution during definition, 213–218

Fairchild (computer company), 14
fairness, and product domination, 169
FDA. *See* U.S. Food and Drug Administration
feedbacks
  architectural competition and, 136–137
  increasing returns world and, 166
  process development and, 79–86
flexibility, and global R&D, 189–190
Ford, 139
Fujitsu, 93, 125, 189–190

Gates, Bill, 157–158
General Motors (GM), 32, 36
Gilder, George, 167–168

Gillette Sensor razor, 86–87
global R&D networks, 171–197
  corporate strategy and, 171, 172–173
  creation of, 175–180
  facility establishment of, 180–190
  initial site leadership and, 181–185
  integration of, 187, 190–193
  management of start-up period and, 186–190
  managerial challenges and, 171–172
  optimal facility size and, 185–186
  qualities of managers of, 172, 181–185, 190–193
  site location and, 178–180
  and sites abroad in 1995, 174
  technology steering committee and, 175–176
  types of sites and, 176–177
global technological parity, 67–68
GM. *See* General Motors
graphical user interfaces (GUIs), 127, 141–142

Harlequin (computer company), 145
harvest phase in architectural competition, 133
health care industry, 55–90

Hewlett-Packard, 18, 86, 154–155, 159, 179, 180, 187
architectural control and, 122, 123, 145
Hicks, John, 152–153
Hitachi, 14, 15
home-base-augmenting site, 176, 177
qualities of initial leader of, 181, 182–185
site location and, 178–179
Xerox and, 193–195
home-base-exploiting site, 176, 177
Eli Lilly and, 195–196
qualities of initial leader of, 182–185
site location and, 179–180
human resources. *See also* teams
cyclical workload mismatch and, 210–213
qualities of leaders of global R&D sites and, 181–185
system-focused *vs.* traditional R&D and, 104, 106–107, 108
Hyphen (computer company), 145

IBM, 93, 152, 162. *See also* DOS
architectural control and, 118, 119, 122, 125–126, 129, 131, 132, 133, 134, 135, 139, 140

AS400, 133
distribution and, 41
ES9000, 98
MVS operating system, 125
organizational strategy and, 32–33, 39–43, 46, 49
OS/2 operating system, 42–43, 142
PCs, 32–33, 40–43, 46, 131, 143, 152, 155
PS/2, 39
RS6000 workstation, 133
System/360, 125
technology integration and, 3, 4, 8, 13, 14, 18
Thomas J. Watson Research Center, 9
ICL (computer company), 93
implementation, and architectural control, 128–129
incentives, and platform product teams, 213
increasing returns
antitrust regulation and, 168–170
competitive advantage and, 147–148
considerations for management in, 166–168
defined, 147, 149
ecological strategies and, 160–162
high-tech economy and, 153–155
management strategies for, 158–163

increasing returns (*continued*)
    nature of knowledge-based
        competition and,
        155–158
    properties of economy and,
        151–155
    service industries and,
        163–165
industrial economies, resource-
    vs. knowledge-based,
    150–155, 165–166
industry standards. *See also*
    architectural control
    architectural controller and,
        120–121
    open systems and, 123–124
    organizational strategy and,
        38–40
    page- and image-descrip-
        tion, 144–145
InfoNow, 138
information flow
    global R&D networks and,
        176, 178, 187–188
    industry standards and,
        38–40
    organizational learning and,
        107–110
    organizational strategy and,
        37–38
innovation, and organizational
    strategy, 35–38, 47–49
integration team
    emergent model and, 10, 11
    system-focus approach and,
        91–92, 94–98, 106–107, 113

Intel Corporation, 86
    80\sd86 microprocessor
        standard, 45–46
    80386 microprocessor, 43,
        132
    architectural competition
        and, 122, 123–124, 126,
        128, 129, 132, 133, 139,
        142, 144
    MMX technology, 221
    Pentium microprocessor,
        221
    platform product definition
        and, 220–221
    Satisfaxion (fax product),
        145
    technology integration and,
        5, 6, 10, 14, 15, 18, 27
    virtual organization and,
        40–43, 45, 51
    xx86 processor, 132, 133
interdependence, and increas-
    ing returns, 160–161
Internet, 4, 24, 153, 159, 160,
    163, 165

Japanese companies
    architectural competition
        and, 119, 128–129
    semiconductor industry
        competition and, 14–15,
        16–18, 19–24
    technology integration and,
        12–13, 14
Java script, 4, 153–154
Jobs, Steve, 142, 159

Johnson & Johnson, 87–89
joint ventures. *See* virtual organization
Joy, William, 33

knowledge-based industries
    compared with traditional
        industries, 148–149,
        150–151, 155–158
    economic regime and,
        151–155
    management style and,
        155–158
    nature of competition in,
        155–158
Korean companies, and semiconductor industry competition, 14, 15, 16, 17,
        19–24

Lexis-Nexis (computer search
    network), 165
Lexus LS 400 (automobile),
    94
lock-in phase in architectural
    competition, 132–133
Lotus, 42, 119, 122, 126–127,
    128, 137
LSI Logic, 119, 122
Lucent Technologies, 179

mainframe development. *See*
    multichip module development
management style, 155–158
manufacturing costs

escalation of, 72–74
process development and,
    74–79
manufacturing process. *See
    also* process development
architectural competition
    and, 128–129
global R&D networks and,
    179–180
market demand
    process development and,
        66–67
    system focus and, 114
market gaps, and platform
    products, 205–206, 212,
        213, 218–220
Marshall, Alfred, 148, 150–151,
    152, 154, 155, 156, 166,
    168
Massachusetts Institute of
    Technology (MIT), 21
Matsushita, 143, 179,
    191–192
McDonald's restaurants, 163
McNeil Consumer Products, 67
mergers, in U.S. semiconductor
    industry, 18
MicroAge, 42
Microcosm (Gilder), 167–168
microprocessors, processdevelopment performance comparisons and,
    17–18
Microsoft, 51
    antitrust case against,
        168–170

Microsoft (*continued*)
  architectural control and,
    122, 126, 127, 131, 132,
    133, 134, 135, 136–137,
    138, 139, 140, 141, 142,
    144, 145
  Excel, 127, 137
  increasing returns and,
    151–152, 153, 161
  Network, 161, 163
  NT system, 134, 136, 139, 142
  technology integration and,
    5, 6, 8, 10, 26
  virtual organization and, 40,
    42–43, 46
  Windows, 43, 124, 127, 137,
    139, 142, 143, 153, 161
  Windows 95, 5, 161
  Word, 127, 137
MIPS Technologies, 44–45, 119
  Advanced Computing Envi-
    ronment (ACE), 44–45
MIT. *See* Massachusetts Insti-
    tute of Technology
Mitsubishi Electric, 93
Moore, Gordon, 27
Moore's Law, 27
Mostek (computer company), 15
Motel 6, 163
Motorola, 15, 18, 122, 142, 172
  organizational strategy and,
    32, 46–49
multichip module develop-
    ment, 93–94, 103–112

National (computer company),
  15

NEC, 14, 93, 122, 179
Netscape, 8, 26, 159
NetWare, 124, 160–161
networks. *See* global R&D net-
    works; user networks;
    virtual organization
NexGen, 18
next-generation products,
    199–222
  customer involvement and,
    207, 217
  cycle mismatch and,
    210–213
  derivative products and,
    205–206, 218–220
  development partnerships
    and, 217–218
  execution during definition
    and, 213–218
  Intel Corporation and,
    220–221
  market gaps and, 205–206,
    212, 213, 218–220
  Orion Computer (fictitious
    company) and, 221–222
  product map and, 203–205
  product strategy and,
    202–207
  project organization and,
    207–213
  resource commitment and,
    201, 213
  sustaining sense of urgency
    and, 214–216
  tracking progress during
    development and,
    214–216

uncertainties and, 202
NeXT workstation, 159
Nike, 45
Nintendo, 129, 143
Novell, 123, 124, 139,
    160–161
novelty, and technology inte-
    gration, 24
NTSC television standard,
    124

obsolescence phase in architec-
    tural competition, 134
Olivetti (computer company),
    118
operating systems, economic
    properties of, 151–152.
    *See also entries for spe-
    cific operating systems*
organizational learning,
    107–110
organizational structure. *See
    also* virtual organization
    architectural competition
    and, 118, 138, 139
    in knowledge-based indus-
        tries, 155, 156–157
    platform products and,
        208–209
    process development and,
        82–86
Orion Computer (fictitious
    company), 221–222
outsourcing, 138–139. *See also*
    virtual organization

Packard Bell, 33

PARC. *See* Xerox, Palo Alto
    Research Center
partnerships with suppliers,
    217–218
PC-DOS. *See* DOS
performance review, and archi-
    tectural competition,
    136–137
pharmaceutical industry
    changing competitive struc-
        ture in, 71–72
    cost advantages of process
        development in, 74–79
    escalation of manufacturing
        costs in, 72–74
    global R&D approach in,
        188–189
    importance of process
        development in, 57–59,
        61–62
    process-development lead
        time and, 79–86
    process-development prac-
        tices in, 68–70
    system-focused R&D and,
        113–114, 115
Philips, 132
pilot production, 80–81
planning. *See* next-generation
    products
platform products. *See* next-
    generation products
Polaroid, 36
positioning
    increasing returns strategies
        and, 162, 167
    process development and, 64

pricing, and product domination, 169
Prime (computer company), 118
Princeton University, 179
problem solving, in system-focused *vs.* traditional R&D, 110–112
process development, 55–90
  benefits generated by, 59–64
  changing nature of competition and, 64–68
  competitive importance of, 57–59
  customer acceptance and, 63
  hard-to-manufacture product designs and, 66
  low-tech products and, 86–89
  manufacturing cost structure and, 74–79
  performance comparisons for DRAM chips, 14–17
  performance comparisons for microprocessors, 17–18
  pilot production and, 80–81
  practices in pharmaceutical industry, 68–75
  prelaunch efforts and, 77–78
  product functionality and, 63
  product life cycles and, 65–66
  proprietary positioning and, 64
  quality of, 79–86
  ramp-up and, 61–63
  shortening lead time and, 79–86
  technology integration and, 5, 6
  technology transfer and, 80
  time-to-market and, 60–61
Prodigy, 159, 163
product development. *See* next-generation products; R&D; system focus; technology integration
product life cycle
  process development and, 65–66
  technology integration and, 4
product map, 203–205
product-priority document, 214–215
product strategy, and platform products, 202–207
prototypes, and platform products, 216–217

quality
  architectural competition and, 136–137
  process development and, 79–86
QuattroPro, 137

ramp-up
  global R&D networks, 177
  process development and, 61–63

system-focus approach and, 104, 106–107

Random House, 52, 53

R&D. *See also* global R&D networks; process development; system focus; technology integration

architectural control and, 128

emergent model of, 10, 11, 12

global approach to, 67–68, 171–197

global technological parity and, 67–68

leveraging capability and, 24–27

product generation gap and, 92

revolutionary *vs.* evolutionary projects and, 24, 25

"Sweet Spot," 97

system-focus *vs.* traditional approach to, 92–93, 98–103

"re-everything," 155

regeneration phase in architectural competition, 134

resource commitment, and platform products, 201, 213

risk-taking, organizational strategy and, 34, 35

Samsung, 14

San Mateo Software Group, 143

Scale and Scope (Chandler), 49

Seagate, 122

Sears, 41

Sega, 129, 143

semiconductor industry

comeback of U.S. companies and, 13–18

models of technology integration in, 19–24

nature of process development in, 27–29

service industries, and increasing returns, 163–165

Sharp, 184

Siemens (computer company), 93, 118, 179, 181

Sigma Pharmaceuticals (fictitious company), 57–58

Silicon Graphics, 26, 44, 143–144

Silicon Valley knowledge cluster, 178–179

Silicon Valley Model

implications of, 139–141

management of architectural competition and, 135–139

Sony, 122, 132

Stanford University, 21, 179

Sun Microsystems, 159

architectural competition and, 122, 123, 124, 129, 130, 132, 134

Java language, 4, 153–154

organizational strategy and, 33–34, 44–45, 46

SPARC, 44–45, 46, 129

Sun Microsystems (*continued*)
SPARC RISC, 130, 132
supplier partnerships, and
platform product devel-
opment, 217–218
system focus, 91–116. *See also*
technology integration
Company A (fictitious traditional company) and,
99–100, 101, 102, 103,
104–106, 109, 110–111
Company B (fictitious system-focused company)
and, 100–103, 105,
106–107, 111–112
integrated problem solving
and, 110–112
integration team and,
91–92, 94–98
as philosophy, 112–115
product-development pro-
cess with, 103–110
traditional R&D approach
and, 92–93, 98–103
systemic innovation, 36–38

Taligent, 142
teams
cyclical workload mismatch
and, 210–213
emergent model of R&D
and, 10, 11
integration, 91–92, 94–98
platform products and,
208–213, 217–218, 219–220
staffing of, 209–210

technology steering com-
mittee and, 175–176
technical concept, 99
technological advancement,
and product domination,
169
technological ecologies,
160–162, 166
technology integration, 1–29.
See also process development; system focus
as challenge for computer
industry, 5–7
change in importance of,
3–5
design of process for, 26
emergent R&D model in
U.S. computer industry
and, 8–12
integration team and,
91–92, 94–98
in Japanese companies,
12–13
semiconductor-industry
performance compar-
isons and, 19–24
successful approaches to,
7–8
technology steering committee,
175–176
technology transfer, and process development, 79–80
technology trends, and foreign
site leadership, 184–185
Texas Instruments, 14–15, 122,
179, 180

3DO (software company), 143
time-to-market, and process
    development, 60–61
Toshiba, 14, 93, 179, 180, 181
Touton, Thomas, 53
Toyota, 45, 140
Tylenol gel caps, 67

uncertainty
    platform products and, 202,
        219
    technology integration and,
        4–5
Unilever, 5–6
Unisys, 93, 118
University of California at
    Berkeley, 179
UNIX, 122, 142
urgency, sustaining sense of,
    214–216
U.S. electronics companies
    global R&D networks and,
        182–184
    technology integration and,
        1–29
U.S. Environmental Protection
    Agency (EPA), 73
user networks, 153–154
U.S. Food and Drug Adminis-
    tration (FDA), 57, 60, 69,
    73, 78
U.S. Justice Department, 168

video games, 143–144
virtual organization, 31–53
    advantages of, 33–35

Ameritech and, 51–53
appeal of, 32–33
autonomous *vs.* systemic
    innovation and, 35–38
balance in organizational
    design mix and, 46–49
factors in success of, 44–46
history of modern corpora-
    tions and, 49–51
IBM PC case and, 40–43
industry standards and,
    38–40
Vistakon, 87–89
Volvo 850, 201

Wang, 130
WordPerfect, 42, 137
Worldview Systems, 52, 53
World War I, 50
World Wide Web, 160

Xerox, 8, 145
    architectural competition
        and, 122, 132, 140–142
    global R&D and, 188,
        193–195
    Interpress software, 132
    Palo Alto Research Center
        (PARC), 9, 141
    Xerox Star, 141–142

Zilog, 128